THE
HARDEST WORK
UNDER HEAVEN

THE HARDEST WORK UNDER HEAVEN

The Life and Death of the British Coal Miner

Michael Pollard

HUTCHINSON
London Melbourne Sydney Auckland Johannesburg

Hutchinson & Co. (Publishers) Ltd

An imprint of the Hutchinson Publishing Group

17–21 Conway Street, London W1P 6JD

Hutchinson Publishing Group (Australia) Pty Ltd
PO Box 496, 16–22 Church Street, Hawthorne, Melbourne,
Victoria 3122

Hutchinson Group (NZ) Ltd
32–34 View Road, PO Box 40–086, Glenfield, Auckland 10

Hutchinson Group (SA) Pty Ltd
PO Box 337, Bergvlei 2012, South Africa

First Published 1984
© Michael Pollard 1984

Set in Linotron 202 Ehrhardt by
Wyvern Typesetting Ltd, Bristol

Printed and bound in Great Britain by
Anchor Brendon Ltd, Tiptree, Essex

British Library Cataloguing in Publication Data
Pollard, Michael, *1931–*
    The hardest work under heaven.
    1. Coal-mines——Great Britain——History——
    19th century   2. Great Britain——Social
    conditions——19th century
    I. Title
    305.9622   HD8039.M62G7

ISBN 0 09 158280 6

'There is no doubt colliers are much harder worked than labourers. Indeed it is the hardest work under heaven.'
  William Wardle, collier of Eastwood, Derbyshire, aged forty, 1841

CONTENTS

LIST OF ILLUSTRATIONS

In the 'thick coal' of south Staffordshire, 1850s (*S*)
Undercutting, 1850s (*S*)

Sources

FWC: From the Rev. F. W. Cobb collection.
NCB: National Coal Board Press Office.
WRO: From the Rev. W. A. Wickham collection, by permission of the Archivist, Wigan Record Office.
JC: John Cornwell.
S: Photocopies from Simonin, *Underground Life*, or *Miners and Mining*.

INTRODUCTION

The British coal industry in the nineteenth century was the finest flower, if that is the phrase, of Victorian capitalism. Commercially, especially in the last half of the century, it was hugely successful. Technically, it was pioneering and innovative. Its leaders demonstrated a degree of business acumen and marketing skill which has rarely been seen in Britain since. As a result of all this – with a measure of historical good luck – the industry managed to position itself at the hub of Victorian industrial enterprise, as the captain of activities ranging from the railway and steamship companies through iron- and steelmaking and metal manufactures even to the lighting of streets and homes. These were all linked not only by their common use of the industry's product, but also by closely interlocked networks of directors, shareholdings, subsidiary and related companies, 'interests', contracts of supply and every other kind of business arrangement from the gentleman's agreement to the cartel; stretching out even into the civil and armed services on occasions, for much depended on, for example, the appearance of a Welsh steam coal pit's name on the Admiralty list or a contract to supply coking coal to the Royal Ordnance Factories. Between 1855 and 1875, coal production in Britain more than doubled. By 1910 it had doubled again.

If one had set out deliberately to design an industry most likely to create class resentment and tension between employer and employed it would have been difficult to find a better model than the coal industry of the nineteenth century. Its pyramidal structure was a grotesque parody of the social structure of the country as a whole. At the top were the owners of coal-bearing land, some 4000 of them, though no more than about two dozen were of any significance in the national picture. Some owners, like the Londonderry and Lambton families in the northeast of England and, on a far more modest scale, the Dowager Countess Waldegrave in north Somerset, involved themselves directly in the mining of the coal beneath their land. But most, like the Dowager Countess's neighbour the Duchy of Cornwall, confined their interest to receiving a royalty on each ton of coal produced. In 1919 the royalties from minerals produced for the Duke of Northumberland a gross income of £82,000, though taxes whittled this down to about £24,000. Questioned about his view of this in front of the Coal Commission, the Duke agreed that he performed no service to mankind in exchange for this income, but complained that he was allowed to keep such a small proportion of it. Ten years before, in the celebrated Limehouse speech which set the entire cast of *Burke's Peerage* trembling, Lloyd George had put the combined earnings of the aristocracy from mineral royalties at £81 million; but then Lloyd George was apt to choose figures more for their impressive sound than for their accuracy, and this would have given an average royalty per ton of about seven shillings, whereas in fact it was more like sixpence. Even so, a more accurate figure for 1909 of about £6½ million was a considerable enough payment for performing no service to mankind. In addition to royalties, landowners received rent for land on the surface and for wayleaves above and below ground, and were, of course, free to let the land above the workings for agricultural or other purposes.

Below the coalowners in the pyramid were the shareholders or partners in the 1500 or so companies which, at the end of the nineteenth century, worked over 3000 pits. Like the owners themselves, these varied greatly in significance, ranging from the large combines like Sir James Joicey and Company, operators by 1896 of twenty-seven collieries in Durham producing between four and five million tons of coal each year, together with shipping and harbour interests, to family enterprises employing a handful of colliers and producing a few tons of coal a week. The operators were the industry's hard men. At the smallest level, they had instincts of the small shopkeeper type and were in any case working on margins too tight to allow decent working conditions or provide decent housing for their colliers. The larger companies, with true capitalist instincts, exploited their workforces without mercy or pity, as for example in the Durham lockout of 1892, just one instance of bloody-mindedness out of hundreds. Coal prices had fallen, and the mine operators demanded a 10 per cent cut in wages. The colliers rejected this, and were locked out for six weeks. With their families starving, the men went back to their employers with an acceptance of the cut, to be told that it must now be $13\frac{1}{2}$ per cent. After a further prolonged stoppage, 10 per cent was finally agreed.

At the bottom of the pyramid were the colliers, who by 1900 numbered over one million. There was precious little to be got out of Victorian industry by those who actually did the work, but colliers were even less well placed than most. It was true that rates of pay tended to be higher than in agriculture or even in equivalent factory work, but this gain was largely lost through the increased cost of living in mining areas remote from towns and markets, and this was identified by at least one commentator as a leading issue in a strike of South Wales colliers in 1871. But when it came to what would today be called job satisfaction, a concept which would have dumbfounded the Victorians although many of them experienced it well enough as an unspoken and unlooked-for bonus, colliers fell way behind other workers. Yarn or cloth from a particular mill, iron from a particular foundry, Middlesbrough sheet or Sheffield wire, had something to say, however quietly, about the practical skills that had gone into producing them. It was not much fun (and indeed it was mucky, fairly hazardous work) making Lancaster oilcloth, but the pictures of Gladstone that adorned so many mid- and late-Victorian kitchen tables reflected skills of photogravure, printing and chemistry that even those on the production line could feel they shared. For those who entered the newly created service industries of the century – the railways, the Post Office, the police, and later the telegraph and telephone services – there was the lure and reward of 'standards' which, with the potentially rapid promotion associated with new enterprises needing to establish qualified middle managements, gave purpose and hope and even a sense of achievement to the lives of those involved. A train delivered to a London terminus on time could win handshakes from first-class passengers. Telegram boys who had travelled miles on a winter's night could expect to be directed below to the cook for a warming dish. Postmen's Christmas boxes were given spontaneously in those days, not as a ransom paid in the hope of prompt deliveries over the next year. But for colliers there were none of these compensations. They made no contribution to the quality of the product, though they might be fined if it contained too much stone. Their work involved no element of service. Although, as was often said, 'once a collier, always a collier', their commitment was perceived only from their side. No one respected them as craftsmen; they were mere, and in many instances literally, hewers of wood and drawers of water. Their only function in the society that their work created was to cut the coal and haul it out of the pits at the pace required by their employers according to the season, the state of trade, and the need to maintain profit margins.

It was true that some pits were more famous than others for the quality of their coal, but this was a territorial rather than a personal acknowledgement. The reputation of Sheffield cutlery was a testimonial, in part, to the cutlers; that of, say, Ashington coal was to geology. However much the colliers' role might be artificially boosted by, from the employers' side when labour was short, grants to colliery bands or male voice choirs or, from the colliers' own resources, by pit banners, it could not be concealed that, in the end, the only reason why men were doing work fit for beasts was that able beasts – or, in many instances, able beasts small enough – could not be found. 'Donkey work it certainly was', recalls one of the former colliers quoted in chapter 3. 'If colliers had been better treated they would have been better men,' said Robert Inglis of Inveresk, aged eighty-two, in 1841. Innumerable observers, doctors, justices of the peace, constables, parish overseers, respectable citizens who wished to remain anonymous, recorded their view of colliers as little more, and in some cases less, than savages. And indeed no one could pretend that to spend eight hours or more a day on your knees, or lying on your side, in mud or water, or pulling a cart to which you were harnessed like a dog (except that the use of dogs as draught animals had been banned) was an occupation likely to encourage an elevated, or civilized, or even less than savage mode of life. The wonder is that so many men, women and children did spend their working lives in this fashion and then came out of the pit at the end of the shift to cultivate flowers, sing Haydn, play musical instruments, learn passages of Scripture, read *Chambers Encyclopaedia*, or make furniture.

'There is a tiredness which leads to stupor which remains with you on getting up and which forms a dull, persistent background of your consciousness,' wrote Nye Bevan, remembering his eight years in the pits. This stupor was enough to keep most colliers away from choirs and flower gardens. 'I am one of the unfortunate class,' wrote Keir Hardie, thirteen years in the pits from the age of ten, 'who has never known what it is to be a child – in spirit I mean. Under no circumstances would I live that part of my life over again.' But for millions it was, of course, the only kind of life they ever had, not only without hope of getting out of it, but often with little chance of ever speaking to anyone who was not serving the same life sentence. The census of 1911 showed that of the 150,000 and more people in the Rhondda Valley, for example, all but about 7500 were either working in or dependent upon the coal industry. This exclusiveness and remoteness made colliers a source of terror, though not wonder, to the 'respectable' population, and this, in the early years of our own century, when through Keir Hardie and others colliers came to have a political voice, gave them a threatening revolutionary tinge that they neither wanted nor deserved. It was not, after all, very unreasonable that on a day in 1894 when, coincidentally, the Duchess of York gave birth to the baby who was to become Edward VIII and some 260 men and boys were killed in a Welsh colliery explosion, Hardie should have suggested that, while the House of Commons moved its customary congratulatory address, Queen Victoria might express her sympathy with the relatives of the victims. But it was seen as an attack from the colliers on the royal family, causing honourable members to wave their order papers, howl, yell and scream. Nearly sixty years later, Harold Nicolson felt that it was, at best, a display of bad taste. 'The member for West Ham, James Keir Hardie,' Nicolson wrote with distaste, 'struck a discordant note. . . . The public and the newspapers were much shocked by this unseemly intervention.' At a distance of ninety years perhaps it may be suggested without fear of accusations of treason that it was indeed more proper for the House to consider the fate of 200 or more people who were in its purview before one, newly arrived, who was not; but, in fact, the proud father found out the truth for himself. In 1912, as George V, he embarked on a tour of industrial and mining constituencies and included South Wales in his itinerary. 'They gave me an extraordinary welcome,' he confided to his diary. 'It was all Keir Hardie's constituency.' Doing his best in a rather mystified kind of way, George V had done something that no previous monarch (no doubt on advice) had dared to do: to go and meet the most terrifying tribe of his subjects and recognize them as fellow human beings. In which he was ahead of the society over which he ruled, to say nothing of that of his grandmother.

1

'FRIGHTFUL FELLOWS AT FIRST SIGHT'

The British Empire, it is said, was built on coal, and the production figures in the relevant period – 7 million tons in 1730 rising steadily to the 1913 peak of 288 million tons – seem to support the claim. Coal fired the furnaces that made the iron from which the cannon were cast, fuelled the ships of Empire's heyday, raised steam for the manufacture of the million products of the world's workshop and became a substantial export in its own right. As early as 1829, Carlyle had the measure of what it was doing and would do: 'The shuttle drops from the fingers of the weaver, and falls into iron fingers that ply it faster. The sailor furls his sail, and lays down his oar; and bids a strong, unwearied servant, on vaporous wings, bear him through the waters. . . . Even the horse is stripped of his harness, and finds a fleet fire-horse yoked in his stead. . . . We war with rude Nature; and, by our resistless engines, come off always victorious, and loaded with spoils.'

Until the eighteenth century, the coal industry was almost a domestic affair, limited partly by scant engineering skills, a relatively small market, the lack of a financial system for raising the substantial capital needed to exploit the deeper, richer seams, and most of all by the amount and unpredictability of underground water. It was the invention of the steam pump that turned coal into a monster, ever more greedy of men, women and children to bore down to it, hole and hew it, load and haul it, lift and sort it; and it was the descendants of Thomas Savery's original machine, the so-called 'Miner's Friend', and their thirst for coal, that drove men into even deeper, gassier, hotter regions. By 1913, Britain was producing a quarter of the world's coal supplies, wrung from over 3000 pits by a workforce of $1\frac{1}{4}$ million, about one in fifteen of the working population. In mining areas the proportion was, of course, much greater. In Northumberland in 1911 one in five of the working population was a miner, and in Durham almost one in three.

By that time, coal had turned large tracts of northern and midland England, east and west Scotland, North and South Wales, into deserts. It had, as Carlyle had forecast it would, strangely altered the old relationships and increased the distance between the rich and the poor. It had created the Labour movement and a whole battery of supporting and rival groupings. It had made dukes and knights, built palaces and whole conurbations of slums, killed hundreds of thousands – nearly 2000 in 1866 alone – and bereaved hundreds of thousands more, crippled plenty by accident or disease. It had made its own mythology, from the legendary Big Hewer with a taste for pickwork no mere man could match, to the compendious Lord Firedamp, a composite of perhaps two dozen titled landowners under whose topsoil the hewers grafted. Coal's sometimes murderous strikers, grieving widows and children, shattered communities deprived of their menfolk by a casual spark, had entered public awareness first through a litany of folksongs and music-hall ballads and later through the popular press. And it had set apart a group of people with characteristics, it seemed, all of their own, as they might be a separate tribe; not like the rest of us, but largely confined – and respectable people thanked God for it – to areas where decent folk need not penetrate. The reports of middle-class venturers into these regions read like those of explorers among undiscovered peoples. The indefatigable Daniel Defoe, travelling in Scotland in 1724, inspected the colliers at Lord Wemyss's pits near Methil in Fife, and noted that 'What with the dejected countenances of the men, occasioned by their poverty and hard labour, and what with the colour or discolouring which comes from the coal, both to their clothes and complexions . . . they are, indeed, frightful fellows at first sight.' An official report of 1842 noted the separateness of the typical pit village: 'Wherever a colliery has been opened a large village or town has been instantly built close to it, with a population almost exclusively of the colliery people, beer-shop people, and small shopkeepers.' If, by chance, there were members of other classes in the vicinity, they made haste to leave, even if they were members of long-established local families. At the opening of a new colliery, a government inspector noted in the northeast of England, 'the erection of long rows of unpicturesque cottages, the arrival of wagons piled with ill-assorted furniture, the immediate importation of the very scum and offscouring of a peculiar, mischievous and unlettered race, the novelties introduced with almost fabled rapidity into the external features of the country, dense clouds of rolling smoke, the endless clatter of endless strings of coal wagons, the baleful colour imparted to the district, are surely sufficient to untenant the seats of the wealthy, and untenanted do they speedily become. The arrival of the pitmen is the signal for the departure of the gentry, and henceforward few indeed visit that district but they who traffic with the coals or the colliers.' The Guests of what was eventually to become Guest, Keen and Nettlefolds, coalowners and ironmasters of the Welsh valleys, built their mansion near Wimborne in Dorset, many miles from a view of pithead gear, and took on a new collective persona as the Wimborne family, owners also of a large tract of deer forest in Wester Ross, another haven from the smoke and smells generated in the course of making their fortunes. Some unfortunates were, however, too committed to move; the Dukes of Hamilton, having built a magnificent palace unwisely adjacent to their workings, and, later having allowed their workings to approach too close to the palace, suffered the indignity of seeing it crumble before their very eyes into the pits that had funded it. 'Subsidences in the park,' *Country Life* reported in 1919, 'have been followed by ominous cracks in the walls. Pick and shovel work nearer and nearer, so that the time seems to be approaching when inhabitance may become not merely disagreeable, but dangerous.' The palace was demolished in the 1920s but, a final irony, the colliery that had wrecked it worked on until 1959. But it was not, of course, as if the Hamiltons had no other homes to go to.

The homes of the collier tribe, too, might have ominous cracks in the walls and distressing signs of subsidence outside, but the tribe had to put up with things. It remained where it was, getting and loading, hauling and winding, riddling and screening, driven in on its own view of the world, such as could be perceived from hundreds of feet below ground or through the murk of the pit bank or the choking dust of the screens. The collier's world was an enduring one, so that even now, in an old mining community which last saw coal won perhaps fifty or more years ago, you can almost smell the oil of the Davy lamps and hear the clatter of boots in the first light; and the first thing you might learn about a schoolteacher or a probation officer or a local government worker is that his father or grandfather was a pitman. Members of the tribe carry their scars with them, sometimes even into NW1 or the leafy Surrey suburbs.

Perhaps some five million people have worked in British pits, many of them from the age of five or six and some – fewer by far – into their seventies and eighties. Most who started in the pits stayed there, women as well as men. Until the 1840s, and in isolated instances later, there were women in their fifties and sixties who had spent their working lives heaving coal underground, ignoring pregnancy, bearing their children at the pit bottom or in the field next to the bank at the end of a shift. As for men, a Welsh doctor estimated in 1842 that the average life expectancy of a collier was about forty; to reach forty-five was rare. It has to be said, though, that at that period this was not so very different from the life span in non-mining industrial or agricultural work; and in Northumberland in the same year there was an ex-collier of ninety-three who had worked until he was eighty-five, having spent seventy-nine years in the pit. He was short of breath, 'but is yet a healthy man on the whole', it was reported. The pits engaged almost the entire working population of whole districts, from their earliest years to their last; they were literally trapped, even those girls and women in areas where, by the end of the eighteenth century, female labour, underground at least, had been outlawed. Colliers married colliers' daughters; there was small chance of meeting anyone from outside the tribe, whose children were in any case not favoured as marriage partners in the outside world. And as for moving away from the coalfields, apart from the physical and financial difficulties pitwork trained tribesmen in no skills that were applicable elsewhere. Few even bothered to think of the possibility; one who did was William Jones of Acrefair near Wrexham in North Wales, but then he was not a collier born and bred. Born in 1799, he started work as a farm servant, and it was not until he was twenty-one that he took to the pit for more money, hauling coal underground for three shillings a day. He found the work hard, and was often frightened and disheartened. He suffered frequent minor injuries and lost his appetite and spirits, but stuck at it for four years until he had saved enough money to buy himself a cart and horse. Married by this time, he made a livelihood for a few years by carting and selling coal, which might be the first stage towards moving away altogether. Living, as he said, 'by sobriety and economy', William Jones deserved to do well, but fate kicked him in the teeth. He built up his business to six horses, but lost them all by sickness, and had to return to the pits. Then, when he was forty-two, he was turned off work. In a way he was luckier than some because he owned his own house; but before he could hope for parish relief he would have to sell it, and his clock, and all but his essential furniture.

There is little enough to be said for the idea that people should earn their living by spending half their lives underground, even under today's conditions which, though not as comfortable as coal industry public relations would suggest, are unrecognizably better in terms of working conditions, safety, health and comparative pay than at any time in the past. Coal mining's history, however, is an affront to human nature, comparable perhaps with the Inquisition. The process of grubbing coal from under the ground required little children to sit down there, usually in the dark, alone for long periods except when a passing collier clubbed them to keep them awake. It required boys, girls and women to be shackled to tubs of coal which they pulled along on all fours. It required men to spend their working days crouched into spaces two feet high or lying on their sides in a few inches of water. It took little account of injury or death. While coal picked off most if its victims in ones and twos – a child dropped from the winding rope here, two hewers caught in a fall of rock there, others taken by one or more of the grim collection of colliers' diseases known commonly as 'shortness of breath' – it could sometimes jump on a community and kick it to pieces. The Oaks Colliery near Bradford blew up in 1866 at the cost of 361 lives. At Abercarn, 268 died in 1878. An explosion killed 290 at the Albion pit in Glamorgan in 1894. Another, at Bank pit in Lancashire in 1910, killed 344. And it was at the Universal pit at Senghenydd – Glamorgan again – in 1913 that Lord Firedamp claimed his biggest recorded prize: 439 men and boys, about half of those underground at the time of the explosion. Nor was he satisfied yet; at Gresford, near Wrexham, in 1934 he picked off another 265.

Lean times or times of plenty made little difference to the miner's lot. Plenty meant greater demand for coal, the working of more dangerous seams, a demand for faster getting, the need to cram more of the young, the infirm and the sick into the pits. Lean times meant the cutting of corners, the ignoring of such safety regulations as existed, cuts in wages, pay-offs. The Universal pit at Senghenydd was being worked flat out at the time of the 1913 explosion, so flat out that there had been no time to put into effect the new electrical safety rules which would have prevented the disaster. By 1934, the coal trade was in the depths of slump, and at Gresford there was an atmosphere of penny-pinching. Men died, either way. And although the colliery company might send white lilies to the memorial service and the local paper might bring out a commemorative issue, the Lord Mayor of London might set up a relief fund and the King might contribute £200, it was usually fairly clear that society could bear such wilful destruction of life with equanimity as, earlier, it had been able to bear slavery. For over 200 years, life or death in the pits were equally cheap.

There was, for example, Anna Hoile, a girl of twelve who worked in a day-hole pit – reached by a horizontal drift rather than a shaft – near Halifax. She had been hurrying – dragging tubs of coal from the working face to the drift mouth – for four years. She didn't like working in the pit, but she had to go because her father had been crippled in his wrists and knees and had to stay at home. No parish relief was available for a man with an able-bodied girl in the family and a wife who could work at home combing wool. Anna went to work at seven in the morning and left at five or six at night. Her breakfast was porridge, and she took a cake to work with her, to eat whenever she got the chance, and had tea and cake when she came home. She rarely had meat. A bleak life; nor was there much to hope for in the way of spiritual comfort. One day she went for the first time to Sunday school. They talked there about God and Jesus Christ, but didn't explain who they were. What they did tell Anna, though, was that if she died a good girl she would go to heaven, but if she was bad she would have to be burned in brimstone and fire.

Robert North started at a pit in Shropshire when he was seven, round about 1830. For the first year he was paid sixpence a day for helping to fill the tubs. Then he was put to driving a horse, and had a mark like a horse's hoof to show for it, among a number of other injuries. Then he took to drawing coal, with a belt round his waist and a chain passing from it, between his legs, to the front of the tub, for twenty pence a day. The chain broke his skin, 'and the blood ran down'. If he complained, he would be beaten – and indeed, when he once did complain, because he was told to draw a tub he knew he could not manage, he suffered two broken ribs as a result. Robert saw and suffered many accidents. He had two fingers broken one time; one more on another occasion. He was singed by gas a couple of times, 'but nothing to hinder me from my work'. But these experiences led him to say the Lord's Prayer twice daily, once at night and once before he went to work: 'When we go to our work,' he said, 'we do not know how we are to come back, whether alive or dead.' At Robert's pit, they were wound down the shaft on the chain, up to ten men at a time with some sitting on the laps of the others. Robert saw a man fall from the chain once. Another time, he saw a man killed by falling coal as he was sitting at his work. And once, Robert lost his way in the workings for two and a half days before he found a place where his shouts for help could be heard.

Then there was William Wardle, collier at Eastwood near Nottingham. He started down the pit in 1810, when he was nine, driving a donkey. When he was eleven he was put to drawing wagons to the pit mouth, eight or nine hundredweight: 'It was very hard work, and I worked at it until I could scarcely stand.' He was beaten till he was black and blue 'with a stick the asses were beat with, or anything they first got hold of; indeed they used no ceremony on that head.' But the pits couldn't do without children – grown-ups would be too big to do the work the children did – and when he had children of his own he sent them both down. Gas troubled the colliers at Eastwood only about once a year; they could tell when it was coming on because it put the candles out, and then everyone made a run for it. At forty years of age, William Wardle didn't think his health had suffered particularly. But there was no doubt that colliers were much harder worked than labourers. 'Indeed,' he said, 'it is the hardest work under heaven.'

The next witness is D. M. Lansley, a retired Welsh collier, and a survivor of the Gresford disaster in 1934. Between him and William Wardle stands a century of legislation designed to make the collier's work safer, healthier and more fairly rewarded. But by 1934 not much had changed, and some of the colliers' gains through union activity had been lost as a result of the failure of the 1921 and 1926 strikes and the prevailing climate of the 1930s, when if you had, or were offered, a job you could take it or leave it. Mr Lansley was working six days a week, eight-and-a-half-hour shifts, for eighty pence a week. You could smell the explosion coming a few years before it actually happened, he remembers, an impression confirmed by, among others, R. E. Edwards, a fitter on the day shift at the time. 'Everyone who worked in the pit,' says Mr Edwards, 'had the feeling that some time, something serious was going to happen. The conditions down the pit, and the heat on working coalfaces was unbearable. But we all had our jobs to do, and no one seemed to grumble; they just accepted it as normal conditions.' Mr Lansley puts it more bluntly: everyone was too frightened of the sack to complain about conditions, he says, and he remembers too that the conclusion of the inquiry following the Gresford disaster was that it was due to unforeseen circumstances. Men who had told the inquiry about the hot conditions and the management's neglect of the pit were not invited back when Gresford restarted; 'Those who spoke for the management did so out of fear, and so told a lot of lies for which they were well and truly compensated when the pit reopened,' according to Mr Lansley. Whatever the official inquiry said, a song written at the time and sung to whip up the relief fund defied the law of libel and laid the blame for Gresford squarely; safety records for the forty-two days prior to the explosion were missing, it said: 'The colliery manager had them destroyed/To cover his criminal ways.'

By 1934, though, coal mining in Britain was in decline. The 'Coal Question', which in its various forms had been haunting the industry for some seventy years – *Was there enough?*, *Was it being won too fast?*, and now, worst of all, *Was there a market for it?* – had come out from political speeches and writing into the open. Almost all naval shipping and about half the world's merchant fleets had converted to oil-burning. Gas and electricity were more economical methods of converting coal into energy, and not only for domestic and industrial use: electrification of the railways had begun. Coal exports from Britain in the 1930s were about half what they had been in 1913. The industry was spiralling downwards; many of the older pits were worked out and could be revived only with massive investment, for which funds were not available. Nothing had been put by during the boom years. For the same reason, the sinking of new pits came to a standstill. By the summer of 1932, 41 per cent of coal workers were unemployed, and by 1938 there were jobs for only 782,000 – a 35 per cent drop from the 1913 peak. Closures in just one coalfield, the relatively small one in north Somerset, illustrate the story: in 1894 there were twenty-seven pits at work, and three new ones were opened before 1914. By the mid-1930s, only thirteen were left, and there was work for only

3500 men compared with the 6500 of 1912. Since the Second World War the national pattern of contraction has continued; in 1981 there were 283,000 men working 220 pits, numbers that have continued their downward drop.

Physically, culturally and emotionally, this decline has been a bitter blow to the collier tribe. Some of the tribal links would doubtless have been cut anyway; in postwar British society, no one who could get a mortgage on a house with a decent bathroom and picture windows wanted to go on living in a two-up and two-down box in a pit row. Some colliers who started off their married life that way were astute enough to snap up their pit houses when the National Coal Board offered them for sale, waiting for a few years and then selling at a price which made a handsome deposit for picture windows. At Grimethorpe, near Barnsley, one of the centres of the British macho-collier tradition, it was said in 1982 that about half the married men were owner-occupiers. With owner-occupation went a different way of life: landscaped gardens, fitted kitchens, pedigree dogs, holidays in the States or Hawaii, even dreams of private education for the children. Face-workers whose fathers wouldn't even bring the coal in from the shed were to be found hoovering, changing nappies, seeing the children off to school. One in six of Grimethorpe's men played golf regularly, some shift workers turning up for a round at dawn. There were still twelve-pint-a-night men to be found, but many others opted for a video in the lounge and a drop of homebrew or even a glass of wine made up from a Boots' kit. These were men who could remember families in their childhood who drank their tea out of jam jars. Men whose fathers' only investments were in the pawnshop now eagerly compare notes on their unit trust holdings. The Miners' Institutes have taken a knock. It was in the 1960s that younger miners started to drink somewhere less rough and ready where they weren't ashamed to take their wives or girlfriends. By the time the institutes started to smarten themselves up a lot of support had been lost. But it's not only the lure of the fashionable that has taken away from the institutes those who can still afford, despite their huge mortgages, to go out regularly for an evening. Many miners no longer need, and indeed now resist, the claustrophobic social life of 'the Welfare', where, as one miner's wife said, 'you're always knee-deep in coal'.

Part of all this can be explained simply by greater affluence and by Britain's national surrender to the consumer philosophy. But it would not have been possible if conditions underground had not altered the colliers' perception of themselves. This change can be put down largely to mechanization. In the first place, this fundamentally shifted the balance of the mining workforce. Mechanized pits – which means almost all of them – demand a high proportion of technically skilled men such as fitters, mechanics, electricians, while haulage by conveyor belt or automatic train does away with the need for the unskilled haulage hand. Boys who, a generation ago, went down the pit at fifteen to work in haulage and learned to be a collier on the 'sitting by Nellie' principle, now, from sixteen, serve apprenticeships – real ones, not the fake pit apprenticeships of Victorian times which were simply a cheap labour device – and attend day-release courses. The second characteristic of mechanization is that it dehumanizes the coal-getting process. A man in his stall – his allotted length of face – with a boy to fill and haul was, up to a point, his own master. If he felt like taking it easy one day, he could do so, and hope to make it up to himself later in the week. Now the machine is master, in the same way as on a production line. The work may not be physically as demanding – though there is still more crawling along low passages knee-deep in water than the National Coal Board likes to admit – but mechanization has brought a new hazard whose effects may not yet be fully known: noise. There was a kind of intimacy about working in a stall that has been lost with the teamwork of the shearer-loader and the conveyor. It would be surprising if this change had not been reflected in the collier's surface life.

But the real damage to the life of mining communities has been done by the fact that many of them no longer *are* mining communities, and many more have become places in which coal mining happens to be one of the occupations. It was noted earlier that in the nineteenth century pitmen had no skills that were of use anywhere else. Although this has become less true with the increasingly technical element in pitwork, it has not been easy for men who have spent half their working lives with coal and colliers to adapt themselves to work in, say, a factory making toys or foam-rubber beds for pets. In South Wales alone the number of wage earners in the pits fell from 120,000 in 1945 to 40,000 in 1970, literally cutting out the hearts of the communities which had been built round the pits a century before. In County Durham, in

1871, there were 160 collieries; in 1983 there were fourteen, and at least four of those had doubtful futures. Too often, the industrial estates set up to provide alternative work are given over to businesses like warehousing with small labour requirements, or to factories needing mainly female labour. Sometimes, there is not even this. The journalist Jeremy Bugler reported in 1972 on a ravaged former mining community, Cambois, on the coast of Northumberland. 'I found,' he wrote, 'a community engaged in a hopeless struggle against the county planners who, reasonably enough, had decided not to allow any new housing in the village because it was a dying community anyway with dreadful housing. . . . The pit had gone, the Co-op had gone, the school had gone, the barber had gone and even the vicar had gone. Only the villagers, growing old, were left behind.' The way the colliers were dropped when their usefulness had been exhausted became the industry no better than the way it had treated them for centuries before.

So the way of life described in this book has largely disappeared, and is as much a part of history as hand-loom weaving or pre-mechanization agriculture. Not so many people, however, will be inclined to be sentimental about the hard labour of the pits as about hand-loom weavers or jolly ploughboys. When Parliamentary Commissions inquired into the conditions under which the Victorians worked in factories, it was possible to contrast these with an earlier period when, according to the romantic myth, the hand weaver worked happily with his wife and family in their picturesque little cottage; and even well into the factory age it was possible to represent the mill girls of Wigan, as in a famous painting by Eyre Crowe, *Dinner Hour at Wigan*, now in the City of Manchester Art Gallery, as living a kind of *rus in urbe* life. The scene is the factory yard, but it looks more like the village pump. One pretty girl, perhaps seventeen, is reading; two more are playing some kind of street game; two more are gossiping; a mother is nursing her baby; and so on. It is a painting interpreting mill-town life in terms that the middle-class patrons can understand, and indeed want to understand. But there were no Friths or Eyre Crowes of the coalfields. Parliamentary sub-commissioners, sent to the pit villages from 1835 onwards to investigate accidents or child labour or working practices, emerged white and shaken, not only by what they had seen but by the difficulty of conveying the horror of it to the legislature. The sub-commissioners were received with suspicion and sometimes hostility, perhaps not surprisingly since many coalmasters had put it about that they were there to see how wages could be cut. Inspecting in the West Riding for the Children's Employment Commission, Samuel Scriven, in 1841, found himself obliged to dissemble: 'All my endeavours to overcome the prejudices that evidently existed in the minds of the colliers proving fruitless,' he reported, 'I determined at once to provide myself with a suitable dress of flannel, clogs and knee-caps, in order that I might descend as many [pits] as possible . . . feeling a conviction that this was the only means of arriving at anything like a correct conclusion as to their actual condition.' John Leifchild, inspecting in Northumberland and Durham, reported similar difficulties, but he did not go so far as to adopt Mr Scriven's stratagem. But this is no doubt the reason why the evidence to the series of Victorian Commissions presents colliers as subdued, often surly, work-weary, resigned to a lot that could never be more than barely tolerable and utterly without pride in their work; in contrast with the miner of the colliers' own folklore, 'a man through and through', as D. M. Lansley wrote to me, 'with a big heart, a man who worked hard, suffered hard knocks, a sociable and kind man, always trying to give a helping hand'.

It is extremely difficult to mine coal – far more difficult than, say, to harvest grain – and the process involves a succession of physically demanding tasks, most of which were, until the beginning of the twentieth century, done by manpower. The coal has first to be cut, and this was almost always, and everywhere, a male prerogative. In south Staffordshire, those who cut the coal were called holers; in south Durham, Northumberland and the east of Scotland, hewers; in Yorkshire, getters; in Cumberland, haggers. It then had to be loaded on to some kind of sledge, or trolley, or wagon, to be taken to the bottom of the pit shaft, or to a point where horses could reach. In some coalfields loaders confined themselves to that function alone, but usually loading was part of the job of the boy or girl or woman or youth who was going to do the pushing or pulling of the vehicle: in Northumberland and Durham putters; in Yorkshire and Cumberland hurriers or trailers, according to whether they pushed or pulled; in south Staffordshire pushers, in the west of Scotland drawers and in the east trammers; and in the north Somerset coalfield, prosaically, carting boys. At the bottom of the pit shaft the coal tubs were hooked on to the winding chain or rope – or, later, wheeled into buckets holding several tubs – by the onsetter or hooker-on, and wound to the surface where they were received by the banksman. At the pit bank there was another army of workers, always less well paid than those below ground and so drawn from those so reduced as to accept any job: crippled or diseased men too sick to go below, the congenitally sick or disabled, orphan children, and, after the employment of small children and women down the pits was prohibited, a greatly increased number of females and boys under ten. Their work consisted of operating the screens separating small coals from the rest, picking out rock, building up the banks of stock coal and loading it into barges or railway wagons.

As the complexities and size of coal-workings increased, so did the hierarchy needed to ensure smooth operation. An eighteenth-century coalowner might typically be a farmer who worked his pit alongside his farming operations, using the same workforce and perhaps even acting as his own banksman, clerk and manager. With the use of coal in the iron industry, and with the development of deeper pits, the management structure inevitably became more complex. An iron company or a colliery company might own a number of pits and appoint a whole management 'tree' to run them; perhaps an overall manager, or 'head viewer' as he would be called in the northeast of England, with an undermanager or deputy viewer for each pit, to run the enterprise as a whole, with an overman and deputies to superintend the works below ground. In the Oldham area the overman was called an 'underlooker', and this is how one colliery manager described his duties in the 1840s: 'The management of each pit is entirely in the hands of an underlooker, who has to keep discipline and regulate all the work, which would be done wastefully and improperly if he did not "keep up" to the men. The underlooker, more or less, goes down every day, at the times of going on work, and afterwards. A good underlooker is not only a good servant to his employers, but much improves the character of the people with him. There are drunken and disorderly underlookers; but generally their character is very different. The employer relies entirely upon the underlooker to see to everything underground where he is the complete representative of his employer.' The underlooker was thus the pivot upon which good practice and safe working conditions hung, and it is not surprising that when at last trade unionism began to take hold in the coalfields, among its first efforts was the struggle to establish a counterbalancing representative of the workforce, initially to ensure that colliers were not being cheated on their earnings by wilful or accidental miscalculation of the amount of coal they had won, and later to improve safety standards.

Though there were local variations, the traditional pattern of working the pits was that the owner or lessee of the land was responsible for providing the means to reach the coal – the shaft, the winding mechanism, the bank equipment, and roads from the pit bottom to the coalface – and the collier for delivering the coal from the working face either to the main road underground or to the pit bottom. A collier working in a rich seam might be able to produce enough coal to keep a couple of loaders – 'fillers', they were called in some places – and two hurriers busy, though there were often local agreements designed to restrain men who were too ambitious. In South Wales, for example, and in parts of Scotland, a limit was placed on how many tubs of coal a hewer might produce, according to the ages of the children he took down with him; in Scotland a child of ten – a 'quarter-bairn' – entitled a man to hew a quarter more than the normal weight allocation, a 12- to13-year-old – a 'half-man' – a half more, and so on. In the northeast of England there was a similar system, based on a scale of 'half-marras' and 'full-marras'.

Unless the colliers were employing their own wives or children for the purpose, they had to pay their loaders and hurriers out of their earnings, and money was also stopped for candles, lamp oil, gunpowder and tools. There was also a fairly comprehensive tariff of fines for offences ranging from delivery underweight, leaving stone in the coal, arriving late at the pithead and dangerous behaviour when being wound up or down to (in some south Staffordshire pits at least) swearing or not joining in prayers. In Northumberland and Durham these fines were paid into a fund for providing relief for widowed and orphaned colliers and for 'smart-money' – compensation for injury – so that although fines were no doubt as bitterly resented there as elsewhere they did not at least represent bare-faced robbery, as in some other places.

Even without the problem of translating earnings into present-day values, it is not easy to make sense of piecework or wage rates in the eighteenth or nineteenth centuries. In general, colliers' earnings were running, through the nineteenth century, at about double those of agricultural labourers in adjacent areas; but these were, in general, the so-called 'high-wage' areas in agriculture, made so precisely by the competition from industry. Certainly it should have been possible – provided that the men of the family could keep off the drink, keep out of debt, and were not struck down by illness or injury – to avoid the worst of the bread-and-gruel existence that was the lot of country families in the south of England. But such comparisons are not particularly helpful, and it is perhaps more useful to look at a number of households in one particular area at one particular time, and see how they fared. John Davis, a collier of Wigan, received £1.10s a week in 1841, and his two daughters brought in another 16s. With this he was able to provide only a house which was 'miserable and wretched in the extreme', with no furniture except for a chair and a rough bench. There was nothing in the house to eat; the cupboard was literally bare. Even less provident was 49-year-old Samuel Bennett, with a wife and four children, three of whom worked in the pit. Between them, he and his three working sons were bringing about £8 a week into the house, most of which was spent on drink. His furniture consisted of a table, two chairs, a squab, three beds ('so called', the report added), and a few pots and pans 'all of the most miserable description'. He had no garden, no cow or pig, and was in no sick society; 'is a good deal in debt, and being in the midst of ale houses and beer shops spends a good deal of his wages in them'.

There were more encouraging stories. Timothy Fairhurst, with two children in the pits and another working at the loom, had £1.6s coming in. He reckoned that he spent about two shillings a week more than this, but nevertheless he managed to provide himself and his family with something like a reasonable home. The Fairhurst family, give or take a few shillings' debt, were just about getting by. But the case of their near neighbour Isaac Mottershead showed that a conscientious and steady young man – he was twenty-nine – could overcome even the condition of having been born into pit life. He reckoned to earn about £1.5s a week, but had managed to save enough to build his own house with a cowshed and garden. He had a wife, who did not work, and two young children. The Mottershead family rarely had butchers' meat, but they occasionally bought a quarter-pig from Isaac's father and salted it down. Milk and butter were provided – with a little extra to sell – by their house cow, and there were fruit and vegetables from the garden. The domestic picture was very appealing: 'In the sitting room is a chest of mahogany drawers, a good eight-day clock in a mahogany case, a good new barometer, a corner cupboard with glass and crockery, two tables and six rush-bottomed chairs, a child's cradle, with fender and fire irons, pictures and chimney ornaments. In the kitchen was a number of earthenware mugs, a table, two chairs and stool, and upstairs was one bed, two chairs, and table; everything was very clean and in good order.' Isaac Mottershead had sensibly protected himself and his family from the loss of this neat and well-provided little home by enrolling in two benefit societies which would, if he were ill, between them provide 17s a week; but in fact there had been no sickness in the house for several years. It is important to remember, in view of what follows, that there were collier families like the Mottersheads, and perhaps it is worth adding that, although their circumstances are quoted from a report on seven families made by the agent of the coalowner, Samuel Bennett was another of the cases cited, as were two other very reduced colliers. The criticism of the coalowners and proprietors must be that, while they would hold up as examples such men as Isaac Mottershead, who had nothing in particular to thank them for, they were prepared to do nothing for those who could not, or whose husbands or parents would not, help themselves.

2
KING COAL

In August 1830 an MP was taken over a pit in Lancashire and recorded the experience in his diary. It was, in fact, a drift, entered by a horizontal adit 'about four or five feet in height, but terrible fatiguing to creep along with bent back and knees'. The seam was about the same thickness, and the layout underground was simple: little more than a few branches leading off the adit into the coal. The hewers worked 'literally without a rag on their bodies', and earned a penny for each three-hundredweight tub drawn out of the pit by 'half-naked little boys' with ponies. Each man reckoned to get thirty tubs a day, but from his earnings he had to pay his drawer and find the ponies' keep.

Ventilation was maintained by an 'upright shaft with a prodigious blazing fire to make a draught up it'. The water was pumped out by hand through the adit, making the entrance very wet. The hewers worked inside rough shelters of props and boards which they moved each time they progressed along the seam. The MP found the men good humoured and intelligent, and they appeared delighted with the penny each he gave them.

This would be a typical pit of the period – a modest enterprise giving work to perhaps two or three dozen people, selling its coal direct in the nearest town (in this case, Padiham), as yet untouched by the age of steam. Such a pit would have only a few years' life. Its owner or lessee would not have enough capital to tunnel far, and it would be cheaper to stop as soon as the easily accessible coal had been won, and start again somewhere else. To sink a shaft was an investment, and implied better prospects; a pit might then become a small family business supporting several successive generations. The grandfather of Thomas Bewick, the engraver, was a farmer near Bywell, about halfway between Newcastle and Corbridge, and, probably about 1700, he opened a pit on his land at Mickley Common. The combination of farming with coalowning seems an unlikely one today, but in fact in the pre-steam age, when the market for coal was almost entirely for domestic use, the two complemented each other well; the demand for harvest labour came at a time when coal sales were at their quietest and many pits closed down for the summer. The Bewicks' colliery continued to support the family at least into Thomas's young manhood – he was born in 1753 – but seems never to have progressed beyond the small business phase. In Thomas's time men were wound down, and water and coal wound up, by horse gin, and his father made a point of attending to the winding of men himself, 'so that he saw that all was safe with his own eyes'. The pit flooded overnight, so that it was often necessary for the first man down in the morning to stand up to his waist or even up to his chest in water, ladling it into the bucket. Mickley Common coal was also sold locally, carters coming from the nearby towns and villages and exchanging gossip over the fire in a bothy, known as 'the Lodge', beside the pithead. Bewick's father seems to have run the pit on fairly informal lines – after a month's or six weeks' work the colliers were allowed to drift off to Newcastle to spend their pay on beer, returning when they were skint – but he could also dispense rough justice: he once extracted a confession from a man he suspected of tampering with the winding rope by threatening to throw him down the shaft.

The earliest mines were either drifts – horizontal tunnels cut into hillsides to reach the outcropping coal – or bell pits. These were similar to the neolithic flint mines at Grimes Graves in Suffolk, consisting of a shaft and a hollowed-out area at the bottom. The workings were reached by ladder or rope, the winding arrangements being similar to those of an old-fashioned domestic well. As the more easily accessible coal was worked out, bell pits became deeper and the horse gin – the first application of technology to coal mining – was introduced. For three centuries or more the horse was to be essential to mining as the means of winding colliers, coal and water, and long after its role on the surface had been taken over by steam it continued to be used for underground haulage.

Bell pits were hopelessly uneconomic. They wasted resources because only the easiest coal – not necessarily the best – was won;

they wasted effort because a disproportionate amount of time was spent sinking new shafts; they wasted capital because the sinker was a skilled craftsman virtually able to name his own price, and one who – unusually in mining – was able to find another market elsewhere, as well-sinker, if the coalmasters' terms didn't suit. By about 1500, Britain's forests had become seriously depleted. Fuelwood was in short supply, increasingly expensive, and protected by legislation designed partly to preserve the hunting forests, but also to conserve timber supplies for the navy. If coal were to fill the gap, it would be necessary to mine it more economically and abundantly, and so it became the objective to work seams out, as far as possible, instead of just nibbling at their edges. Parallel roads were driven from the shaft bottom into the seam, and crossroads, known as 'bords', were driven at intervals at right angles. Coal was then cut by the 'room and pillar' system, building up a network of parallel roads, the intervening blocks of coal – the pillars – being left to support the roof. This system allowed colliers to venture further away from the shaft until either ventilation or underground water made further work too difficult.

By 1700, about the time the Mickley Common pit was opened, coal production in Britain had reached about $2\frac{1}{2}$ million tons a year, about twelve times what it had been 150 years before, and it was becoming clear that this was likely to be its ceiling unless a solution could be found to the problem which had become pressing with the extension of room and pillar working. This was underground drainage. The amount of water at the depths now being explored was beyond the capacity of relays of small children armed with buckets, hurrying between working face and shaft bottom, and of the primitive winding arrangements of the time, to deal with. Working to the rise – that is, uphill – the water drained away naturally, but to the dip (and colliers could no longer afford to confine themselves, for the sake of convenience, to the easier working) it was necessary to provide drainage channels. As the underground workings became more extensive, this became more difficult. In some pits water was permanently knee-deep on the underground roads, with more literally spouting out of the roof and, in other places, falling, as one observer put it, 'in great drops like the shower of a thunderstorm'. Lying on their sides to pick at the coal, hewers might have their lower legs immersed in water. Where horses were used underground they were sometimes provided with waxed cloths over their backs to give them some protection, but as for the men, it was often necessary for them to come up two or three times in each shift to change into dry clothes. Within a few minutes, on their return below, they would be soaked again.

The first hint of a solution came in 1698 when a Devon man, Thomas Savery, invented the crude steam-operated 'water-raising engine' which was patented as the 'Miner's Friend'. It was, truth to tell, a fairly unsatisfactory device with a tendency to blow up if put under strain, as one did when it was tried out in a Staffordshire pit where it was expected to pump water from over 100 feet down. But Savery's engine did at least draw attention to the possibility of pumping water by means of steam pressure, and it inspired a near neighbour of his, the Dartmouth blacksmith and ironmonger Thomas Newcomen, to design a simple beam engine which was the forerunner of the thousands of machines which, though much improved by James Watt, Matthew Boulton and others, were to be the workhorses not only of mine drainage but also of winding operations for nearly two centuries. Like Savery's, Newcomen's engine was a prodigious user of fuel, which was a drawback to its use anywhere but at pitheads; here, however, its popularity spread rapidly, especially since it was not fussy and would work on coal so small or low grade as to be unfit for the market. The first Newcomen engine to be used for pumping water out of a pit was installed at Congyre, near Dudley in Staffordshire, in 1712, seven years after Newcomen registered his patent, and over the next twenty years it was followed by about 100 others. Though more reliable than Savery's, the 'common engine', as it was popularly called, lacked a safety valve and could be dangerous left to an inattentive engineman; and it ran very erratically, which was not too much of a problem with a simple task like pumping water, but made it unsuitable and unsafe for winding coal or colliers. Nonetheless, Newcomen engines were used for winding in Ayrshire pits until the mid-nineteenth century. Boulton and Watt's improved version, patented in 1769, was more reliable and used only about one third as much fuel, and it was this or its many imitations that provided the first mechanical winding on any large scale, though the Newcomen engine retained its popularity and indeed superiority in the coalfields until after 1799, when the Boulton and Watt patent, which had been extended by act of Parliament, finally ran out. It was discovered that some of the jerkiness of the Newcomen engine could be evened out by using the water it pumped up to turn a waterwheel which provided power for winding, and this method was widely adopted in the northeastern coalfields from the early 1780s onwards. During the closing decades of the eighteenth century and the first of the nineteenth the landscape of coal-mining areas was changed substantially and enduringly by the erection of the familiar pithead gear: the wheel, set in its trellis of scaffolding, and the adjacent engine house. The work of Newcomen and his successors is the main reason why coal production in Britain was able to double between 1700 and 1750, and double again by 1800. And in the succeeding century, of course, the development of the stationary engine into the locomotive was to spur even greater increases in production as Britain steamed towards her reputation as the workshop of the world.

Meanwhile, in 1709, Abraham Darby had made the first of the moves which were to revolutionize the iron industry and, again, to have an enormous impact on coal. At Coalbrookdale in Shropshire he built the first blast furnace successfully to smelt iron using coal rather than charcoal. The notion of this had been about for a long time, but the persistent difficulty had been the impurities in coal; Darby's contribution, which changed the scope and nature of the ironmaking industry and within forty years made the Coalbrookdale area Britain's leading iron producer, was to coke the coal first. This created a huge new market for coal, and one that was not seasonal.

It was the vast, uncontrolled expansion of these years that led to some of the worst abuses of the coal industry. It created an intense and sudden shortage of labour, increasing the pressure on women and children to go down the pits or work on the pit banks. Rapid growth created a housing shortage which was met by squalid solutions: jerry-built cottages, gross overcrowding, the keeping of run-down lodging houses. Increased numbers at work in the pits, and the rush to get them there in time to work a full shift, made winding a more hazardous operation, especially when the tending of the horse gin or the engine was left to young boys.

The sudden and accelerating demand for coal put in jeopardy the older, safer working practices. The original form of room and pillar working left substantial pillars in place, partly for safety but also to prevent subsidence. Indeed, mineral leases often provided for the laying aside of topsoil at the opening up of a new pit and complete restoration of the site when operations ended, but this was a piece of early concern for conservation which was speedily dropped once the real race for coal was on, with results that are still only too obvious in many old mining areas. Given the new conditions and the new hunger for coal, it was no longer thinkable to leave the pillars untouched, and so the process of carving them away – 'robbing the pillar' or 'working in the broken', colliers called it – began. At first, the pillars were made only slightly smaller, but as the temptation of the easily won pillar coal increased the depredations became greater. The stresses set up in the pillars and in the roofs and floors of the roadways were unpredictable, and when a pillar was being robbed anything could happen. Ironically, or perhaps it was a kind of rough justice, much of the coal gained by this method often broke down into small coal or slack, fit only for the pit's own engines, because of the pressures it had been subjected to. Propping was expensive and the time spent doing it non-productive, so it was often skimped, while there was always that spine-chilling moment when the props were finally knocked away from workings about to be abandoned. Roadworks in the 1980s in parts of the old Fife coalfield, which have involved exposing room and pillar workings, have shown just how risky pillar-robbing operations became. Pillars were found which were as little as four foot square, at intervals of eight to twelve yards. The standard safety test for colliers working in the broken, which itself sounds fairly risky, was to strike upwards at the roof with a pick. A clear ring traditionally meant that it was safe, but this could sometimes be deceptive because if the roof was broken into large blocks it took a very discriminating ear to tell the difference. Later, in room and pillar operations, robbing the pillar followed closely on the pillar-making cut, thus reducing the opportunity for unpredictable stresses to be set up, giving better coal and slightly safer working conditions.

By the 1830s it was only the older pits, and those closing fast, that were worked on the simple lines of the Bewick pit at Mickley Common, with the coal being carted away to be sold locally as soon as it was brought up. The huge and constant demands of industry, especially the iron industry and the potteries, the spread of canals and railways and the consequent better organization of distribution, the demands of the market for coal of specific standards and the sheer volume of operations had combined to turn the pithead area into a scene of activity almost as intense as that underground. Driving the horse gin was traditionally a boy's job, though it occasionally went to a girl or an old woman. Work on the bank – tipping the skips of coal as they were brought up, hooking empty skips on to the winding chain, sorting rock from coal, or wailing as it was called in the North – was done by boys or girls, but notably girls, even in areas like south Staffordshire where, by the end of the eighteenth century, none were employed below ground. Loading canal barges with coal from the banks was also, in Staffordshire and Derbyshire, often a girls' job. There were sound reasons for employing girls on surface work. The coalmasters were responsible for paying surface workers, even in areas where underground work was subcontracted, and so wages were poor. Boys wanted, if possible, to get below where the better money was, and eventually to become members of the pit aristocracy as hewers. In south Staffordshire in the 1840s, a boy driving the horse gin was paid sixpence a day, whereas underground he would have been paid five shillings or more a week with the prospect of steady advancement until, at seventeen or so, he would be receiving fourteen shillings. In the west of Scotland rates for underground work were about double those on the surface. In Northumberland and Durham a putter underground could earn about two shillings a day, but one shilling to one-and-six was the price for 'various desultory work at the top of the pit, such as taking out stones, carrying the picks, tramming out the screens, firing the engine, assisting the banksmen, etc.'. The government inspector who in 1841 reported on the south Staffordshire coalfield, Dr Joseph Mitchell, was refreshingly realistic about the employment of girls and women above ground. Commenting on the young bankswomen, who were 'generally singing at their work, and always appear smiling and cheerful', he wrote: 'There are some persons who object to girls being employed in outdoor, and what is supposed to be laborious employment, but when we consider how many employments men have engrossed to themselves, and how few ways there are for women to gain their living, we must be cautious not to attempt to narrow what is already so limited.' There was a good point here. In the north Somerset coalfield, where pitwork was entirely male, and there was no alternative employment such as spinning or weaving for the women, the standard of living was correspondingly low in the first half of the nineteenth century, though gloving and the boot trade brought opportunities for women later. Twenty years after Dr Mitchell, a writer in the *Edinburgh Review* was taking a similar line that bankswomen – as distinct from those who worked underground – were cheerful, knew plenty of songs, and liked a joke. 'This is heavy and dirty work,' he wrote, 'and the pitgirls who are engaged in it, with their shabby dresses tied grotesquely about them, and their inverted bonnets stuck on the top of their heads, seem not less sordid. But before the philanthropist draws his conclusions, let him see them on Sunday (we wish it were an equivalent phrase to say at church), with clean persons, bright complexions, sparkling eyes and dressed out in the cheap finery which nowadays levels all distinctions of costume. . . . Much may be done to improve the conditions of the poor pitgirl, but it would be an ill beginning to deprive her of her bread.' But this was by no means the universal view of bankswomen. Their work, wrote H. S. Tremenheere, the first (and, in the beginning, the only) permanent government inspector of mines, in 1856, was 'one degrading to the female character. The kind of attire rendered necessary by the masculine nature of the employment, and the blackness and dirt with which these females cannot avoid being covered, can scarcely fail to undermine their modesty and self-respect, while it is notorious that their association with the coarse description of men employed in that branch of labour exposes them to every deteriorating influence of language, manners and habits.' It was as well that the sensitive Mr Tremenheere did not make the acquaintance of jolly Mary Glover, a 38-year-old drawer in a pit at Ringley Bridge in Lancashire, who told one of her colleagues that although she insisted on wearing a good pair of trousers, 'I have had many a twopence given me by the boatmen on the canal to show my breeches.'

The temporary ascendancy given to the coal industry of Shropshire and the west Midlands by Abraham Darby's coke smelters was soon eclipsed by developments in the northeast, stemming directly from the use of steam. A new generation of deep pits began to be sunk along the Tyne, beginning with the Walker, east of Newcastle, in 1765 and reaching a peak in the first decade of the nineteenth century with the opening of Percy Main near North Shields (1802), Jarrow (1803) and South Shields (1810), all over 600 feet deep. The increasing area of underground workings served by one pair of shafts (or, in some cases, by one single shaft) exacerbated the difficulties of ventilation, especially as the deeper the workings, the more vulnerable they were to gas. The period between the sinking of deeper pits and the introduction of the safety lamp – some fifty years – put all who worked in the pits at risks which are horrifying to contemplate. The threat in earlier times had been mainly from carbonic acid gas, called by the colliers 'chokedamp' or 'blackdamp'. The danger here was from suffocation, but the collier normally had warning because chokedamp put his candle out. Carburretted hydrogen gas – wildfire, 'sulphur', or firedamp to the collier, methane or marsh gas to the chemist – was found in the deeper seams and was altogether more threatening. At one part to fourteen of atmospheric air, carburretted hydrogen gas is explosive, and its volatility increases to the ratio of one to seven or so, after which the risk diminishes. At one to thirty an observant collier could detect the gas because at that strength it would enlarge the flame of his candle, but the safety margin was slender and the opening of a new joint in the workings could suddenly release quantities of gas without warning. Until the introduction of fans, pits were ventilated by a furnace – the 'prodigious blazing fire' seen by the MP quoted at the beginning of this chapter. This was placed near the bottom of the upcast shaft, and drew fresh air through the workings from the downcast shaft. (Until the provision of two separate shafts became mandatory after 1862, one shaft was often used for both purposes by dividing it into sections with airtight shuttering or 'bratticing', as it was called.)

Matthias Dunn was the manager of Hebburn Colliery on Tyneside in 1810. It was a fairly new pit, having been opened only sixteen years, but it was nevertheless 'accounted the most dangerous in the trade', according to Mr Dunn. Between the downcast and upcast shafts, the air travelled thirty miles underground through the room and pillar workings, its route determined by stoppings and shuttering built across the bords. Eventually things got so bad that the return air caught fire when it reached the ventilating furnace. As the safety lamp had not yet been invented, there were only two possible forms of lighting: candles, which were simply unsafe in such conditions, or steel spark mills which produced a stream of sparks when thumbed. These 'produced barely sufficient light to travel with in safety', and after trying various schemes to exhaust the pit of its gas Mr Dunn concluded that it was utterly impossible to work it either safely or profitably. There had already been one explosion in 1805 which killed thirty-five men. But after two years there was a return to work, and in 1814 another explosion killed eleven. As will be seen in a later chapter, the inventors of the safety lamp, whatever their humanitarian intentions (and these are open to doubt), did a disservice to the mining community by making it practicable to work pits like Hebburn while to some extent concealing the danger. In 1825, after the Davy lamp had been adopted, four men were killed by a gas explosion. Two more died in 1830 and another three in 1836.

The ventilation problems of deep mines were the main reason why Northumberland and Durham stayed with room and pillar working, despite its waste of resources, rather than adopting the longwall method, which had become increasingly popular elsewhere by the early nineteenth century. The original longwall practice was to start working from the shaft between two parallel roads, taking out all the coal. The space from which the coal had been taken was propped, and as the work advanced this space, which was called the 'gob' or 'goaf', was packed with stone, small coal and rubbish. Props were inserted to support the new face, the old ones were knocked away and the roof was allowed to collapse. This kind of working was called 'advance longwall', and its disadvantage was that it cut off the colliers from the shaft bottom by an area in which rock falls might occur or dangerous accumulations of gas could build up; it also steadily increased the distance over which coal had to be hauled to the shaft bottom and so made it difficult to determine and control prices. A more satisfactory version of longwall working is the retreat system, in which roads are driven out from the shaft to the full extent of the coal to be worked, and the coal is then cut back towards the shaft. This system was in use here and there at the turn of the twentieth century, but it is only since nationalization that it has been fully developed. This is partly because it is particularly well suited to the full-scale mechanization of today, but the slowness of the industry to adopt it earlier was due to its one great disadvantage in capitalist terms: the huge investment required to drive the roads forward and equip them with rails had to be made long before there was any income from output.

It was never easy, when collieries were in private hands, to find investors, and this is why during the nineteenth century, when capital was needed for the new technology and to meet the increasing call from governments for expensive safety measures, the industry tended to be concentrated into fewer hands. It cost about £50,000 to sink the Hetton Colliery in east Durham in the early 1820s, and in the same area Murton Colliery, in the same period, soaked up £250,000 before it began to show a profit. This was not the kind of money likely to be found by many people in the industry, especially when, as at Haswell, also in Durham, £60,000 might stand to be written off without the hope of a penny in income. The latter half of the nineteenth century is notable for the increasing interest in the mining industry of 'big business', and by the end of the century the most productive and efficient pits were being operated by combines like Powell Duffryn and the Cambrian Trust in Wales, the Fife Coal Company and United Collieries in Scotland, and, in England, the Charlesworths Briggs and James Joicey companies. The last was particularly significant, because in 1906 it signalled the tendency of the aristocracy to depart from coalowning when James Joicey bought up not only Lord Durham's collieries, but also his steamships, giving the firm control of twenty-seven pits and fifty steamers.

It was not only that the operation of the pits itself was becoming more capital intensive; new coal was getting more difficult to find and prove. As the North Yorkshire coalfield, for example, spread eastwards towards the Great North Road, its pits grew steadily deeper: 1320 feet at Glasshoughton, near Castleford, in 1870; 2148 feet at the Prince of Wales pit near Pontefract two years later; 1638 at Fryston in 1875; 1728 at Ackton Hall, near Featherstone, in 1888. Prospecting was expensive and frustrating, too. In the early years of this century the Earl of Londesbrough, the major landowner in the Selby area, commissioned a series of deep boreholes on his land, following the logical conclusion that the rich Barnsley seam which the pits just mentioned had been sunk to exploit, must be down there somewhere. His surveyors tried in 1904, and in 1909, and again in 1913, without success. Selby coal was to remain undisturbed for another fifty years. But even if the Earl's surveyors had found the seam, which is, in fact, about 2500 feet down, it is unlikely that he would have been able to raise the funds to exploit it. It was round about this time that the Kent coalfield, Britain's youngest, was being developed, and the story was one of constant dicing with collapse.

Coal had been discovered in Kent in a curious way. When, as the result of a Commons Select Committee decision, work was stopped on the English side of the Channel Tunnel in 1882, test boreholes were made, almost as a matter of academic interest, in the tunnel opening at Shakespeare Cliff near Dover. A number of seams were found, and a well-subscribed company was formed to develop them. A fair amount of money seems to have been spent with very little result, but in the meantime another company had begun to explore the area north of Dover and, despite the scorn of the City, where 'Kent coal' became a Stock Exchange joke, was able finally to open up the coalfield, having overcome considerable obstacles to the investment involved.

However, when we hear that there were well over 3000 pits at work in Britain in the nineteenth century it must be remembered that almost all of them were nearer in scale to Mickley Common, doomed to close as diminishing resources and advancing technology made them uncompetitive, than to the big business ventures of the last great decades of coal supremacy. The reason why so much of the British coal industry had such a shoestring look, which persisted until nationalization in many places, was the lack, in the early days, of the kind of entrepreneur who was responsible for the rapid development of railways. When, in 1810, the first meeting was held to discuss what turned out to be the Stockton and Darlington Railway, the chief promoter of the idea, Edward Pease, had little difficulty in attracting the interest of investors, but no one at that time could have been found to invest the same kind of money, time or interest into such a proven business idea as a successful working coal pit needing more equipment. What happened at Ridings pit near Stanton Drew in Somerset was typical of the shaky foundations of many colliery companies. It was opened by four partners in 1808; some capital must have been found in the beginning at least, for it had both a pumping engine and a winding engine at a time when the latter was by no means universal, especially in the archaic Somerset coalfield. But the venture was beyond the experience of the partners from the start, and it was to be dogged by ill luck. Two of the partners died and their shares passed to their families, who had no more capital to offer and, it seems, very little interest in the business. The pit blundered on inefficiently and unprofitably for some years, but in the 1830s the partnership was wound up when water flooded into the workings, a circumstance that had been inevitable from the beginning. But it took courage, perhaps fool's courage, to sink any money into the Somerset coalfield in any case; it was always hampered by its remoteness from the big industrial markets, by lack of communications – one colliery had a rail connection from 1854, but the others had to wait until the Bristol and North Somerset and Somerset and Dorset lines arrived in the mid-1870s – and simply by lack of marketing expertise. In a rather lackadaisical way, the coalfield sold its output in Bath and in the Mendip towns and villages, involving, in the case of Mendip, two- and three-day carting over atrocious roads, and failed even to break into the more hopeful Bristol market only a dozen miles away. It was not until after the railways came that the coalfield produced more active owners and lessees who positively went out to seek new markets and, for example, challenged the railways' high freight charges.

By contrast, the direct landowning interests in the Tyneside pits brought the management skills of land agents and the technical ones of surveyors into play fairly early on, while the owners themselves combined with the shipmasters of Newcastle to form a powerful marketing force to sew up the London trade and fight off competition with agreed prices. This was a context more likely to stimulate innovation and improvements. Screening was introduced in Northumberland in the 1760s to separate out the small coal and so produce a more standardized product which could command a premium price. The first experiments in the use of cages for winding coal and colliers were carried out on Tyneside in the years before 1820, though it was another twenty years before cages came into general use even there. It was no accident that the thrusting northeastern coalfield, greedy for productivity and results, produced men like George Stephenson, who taught himself reading, writing and subsequently engineering, while tending the pumping engine at Wylam and Killingworth pits. In the large pits there was scope for promotion, and engineering skills could command a high price; as the engineer at High Pit, Killingworth, Stephenson had a salary of £100 a year in 1812, when he was thirty. It was remarkable for the son of a colliery engine fireman to achieve international eminence, as Stephenson did, but there were many stories of lesser, though considerable, advancement from the northeast. The climate was right there for men who could master the new techniques, and manage the newly inflated workforces, to prosper. One such was William Brown, the son of a collier who became a colliery manager and subsequently part-owner of a number of pits. Another was Sir George Elliott, born in 1815, working in the pit at nine, underground manager at twenty, part-owner of a colliery at twenty-five, owner at forty-eight of the colliery where he had started work, and later owner of mining interests in Wales, Staffordshire and Canada, shipowner, MP, baronet and deputy lieutenant of Durham. There is a portrait of this ambitious and successful man in the form of the evidence that he gave to the Children's Employment Commission in 1841 when, aged twenty-seven, he was the manager of Monkwearmouth, Belmont and Washington Collieries, the last of which he part-owned. He had given some thought to the problem of trapping, and considered that little boys could be dispensed with and replaced by a mechanism applying to air doors in pits; the same principle used in level-crossing gates. The idea had come to him at an exhibition of railway gates held the year before at the Polytechnic in Newcastle. Unlike many of his colleagues, he was in favour of schools where religious and moral instruction were given, and he approved of the Methodists although he was not one himself. They had, he said, 'done more to ameliorate the pitmen than the whole church put together'. Although when he came to eminence he espoused staunch Conservative principles, the strain of liberalism discernible in the man of twenty-seven remained with him, and Sir George was one of the few shipowners for whom Samuel Plimsoll had a good word to say. For all that, though, the fortune that Sir George made was founded, like the huge incomes of Lord Durham (£84,000 in 1856) and the Duke of Northumberland (£82,450 in 1918), on human misery. There was, for example, 16-year-old Nichol Hudderson, at work in the Monkwearmouth pit at the same time as the future Sir George was giving evidence to the Children's Employment Commission. What job Nichol did in the pit is not clear; probably he was a filler. He should have been putting, but an accident the year before, when a runaway horse dragged him along in its traces, had shortened one of his legs. He had been six years in the pit, in bad health the whole time. The heat made him sick, and the sulphur fumes made him dizzy. He left home at three in the morning, and sometimes, depending on how far it was from the shaft bottom to where he was working, didn't get home until seven at night. Sometimes he was too sick to be able to eat his bait in the middle of the day; sometimes he brought it up again. When he got home he was often too tired to eat or do anything but lie down by the fireside. It might sound as if Nichol were piling on the misery, but there was plenty of corroboration from others in the same pit. Richard Bell, thirteen, also complained of sickness and dizziness – and of his treatment by the overseer, who frequently flogged him and had once hit him so severely over the head with a stick that he had been off work for two days. James Johnson, sixteen, horse driver, complained of sickness, which sometimes prevented him from eating his bait, and also of boils the size of a hen's egg on his legs and under his arms, brought on by the salt water and the heat. The pit made John Bell, driver, bring up his food three or four times a fortnight, and it was the same for 14-year-old John Dickson. Of forty-five other boys interviewed, almost all complained of the heat and of sickness. But Dr W. J. Dodd, employed by the owners, had never heard of any boys complaining of the vomiting of food down the pit, though 'this might be naturally expected in some cases the result of ascending and descending smoky upcast shafts'. George Elliott agreed that boils were a problem at Monkwearmouth, and had suffered himself. He put it down to the excessive drinking of spring water in the pit. He added that the colliery was 'quite an asylum for asthmatic people'. It could hardly have been anything else. Asthma was one of the most commonly mentioned occupational ailments, following bronchitis and what was then diagnosed as phthisis but was in fact pneumoconiosis or, as the colliers called it, 'black spit'. Almost every collier without the good fortune or application of George Elliott or William Brown was condemned, even if he survived accidents, to a wasting death, probably by the age of fifty or so.

At birth, collier children had as much chance as anyone else, perhaps more, because difficult births seem to have been comparatively rare among collier women and miscarriage or stillbirth, which were frequent, weeded out the weaker specimens. 'But before they have lived many weeks,' reported a leading physician in 1841, 'a remarkable inferiority is observable, especially to the children of farm labourers, and of other individuals in comfortable and respectable circumstances.' Poor food, overlong suckling (in Scotland, often to the age of two), exposure to overheating and poor ventilation and generous dosing with Godfrey's Cordial – a mixture of treacle and opium – or the even more poisonous Dalby's Carminative (magnesia, tincture of asafoetida, pennyroyal water and opium), soon began to eat away at good health. Add to this intake of opiates frequent spoonfuls of gin or whisky for digestive purposes, and it is not surprising that, as one doctor remarked, 'medical men seldom see the children until they are benumbed and stupefied'. Those children who survived all this went into the pit or on to the bank, where they were exposed to further hazards. 'About the age of twenty,' wrote the physician quoted earlier, 'few colliers are in perfect health, almost all being more or less affected with difficulty of breathing, cough, and expectoration. . . . The body of the adult collier at this age is generally spare, the muscles and sinews being well developed, and well marked in their outlines. . . . The women at this age are in general healthy, muscular, and not deficient in fat.' But, he went on, between twenty and thirty the men declined in strength and their breathing became more laboured: 'This period is fruitful in acute diseases such as fever, inflammation of the lungs and pleura, rheumatic fever, and many other ailments.' From then on, for most, it was downhill all the way. He reckoned that only one in fifty 30-year-old collier males would have been found medically fit for the services (and at that time the forces would take almost anyone who could stand up straight). In the thirties, debilitation set in; in the forties, there was a rapid decline in health: 'The symptoms of decay now succeed fast, and death is busy in the selection of his victims.' Those who got past fifty were for the most part husks of men. A government inspector said of colliers in the West Riding that 'after they are turned forty-five or fifty they walk home from their work almost like cripples, stiffly stalking along, often leaning on sticks, bearing the visible evidences in their frame and gait of overstrained muscles and overtaxed strength'.

Relatively few colliers in the nineteenth century survived to die of 'black spit' itself, although it was, in the end, inevitably fatal. The symptoms were emaciation of the whole body, constant shortness and quickness of breath, occasional stitches in the side, quick pulse, and a hacking cough day and night 'attended by a copious expectoration for the most part perfectly black'. Breath wheezed in the bronchial tubes, the muscles of respiration became prominent, the neck shortened and the chest drawn up. These were men who were literally fighting for breath. But what killed them more often than 'black spit' itself was their vulnerability, because of their reduced condition, to bronchitis, asthma, or whatever else might be about.

The colliers observed by the West Riding inspector, shuffling home from work like cripples, were very far removed from their own self-image as reflected in their folklore. The hewer in pit mythology was the tireless giant, the man with the strength of ten, the Derby Ram of the coal pit. In south Staffordshire he was called Dick the Devil and worked only at night when no one else was about. In South Wales he was Big Isaac, who cut anthracite with his teeth while he held up the roof with one hand. In Derbyshire he was called Jackie Tor, and in Durham Bob Towers. 'He couldn't be beat,' said a Durham miner of Bob Towers. 'By, he was a big man. Can you imagine? He was eighteen stone – no fat, eighteen stone of man; what we called the County of Durham Big Hewer. He was like a machine when he was hewing. You could hear the pick, pick, pick, pick, as regular as the clock. He never used to seem to tire.' In real life the hewer's, or holer's, or hagger's, or getter's job was not to go at the coal like an automaton, but to undercut (in some coalfields he was called the 'undergoer') a seam to a height of about two feet, double propping as he went and clearing the cut coal behind him to be collected by the fillers. The further line of props was then knocked away and, with luck, the rest of the seam would fall. If not, a wedge might be driven in at the top to help it on its way, or explosives – in the old days, gunpowder – might be used. It was a job involving timing and judgement as well as nerve, physical strength, muscle and sinew. In thin seams such as those of Shropshire, two feet or less, all the coal except for the pillars might be literally hacked out, the hewer crawling as far as fifty feet into a space too narrow to do more than wriggle in. The practice in the Midlands was for the hewer to work on his side, whereas Northumberland and Durham men worked on their hams, which permanently bowed their legs. The usual posture in the west of Scotland was with one leg doubled underneath and the other foot against the coal, bending the body almost to the ground to wield the pick.

It was worst in the thinnest seams. In Lancashire, a collier was found in a seam eighteen to twenty inches deep sitting doubled up, his chest almost resting on his thigh and his head bent almost to the knee – 'but it was curious to see the precision and smartness with which he dealt his blows,' added the report. It was common in the West Riding to find men working lying their whole length on the uneven floor, supporting their heads on a board, or sitting on one heel with the other extended to balance themselves. In room and pillar working, the moment of robbing the pillar gave some relief from these agonizing positions; for this, the men stood with prickers, long-handled tools with a point and a hook at the end with which to jab and tear at the pillar until it was judged that collapse was imminent. 'At last a cracking is heard,' reported an observer of this activity in south Staffordshire, 'and the miners run off as fast as they can, and happy are they if all escape unhurt by the fall of the coals.' But a collier spent most of his working life crouching, lying, kneeling or, at best, sitting in a confined space, and it was not surprising that deformities of the legs, the spinal column and the shoulders were commonplace.

Face-working was the last aspect of mining to get relief from hard labour by the use of machines, mainly because of the difficulty of finding a safe source of power for underground work. In 1850, compressed air was first used to drive a pit engine – for haulage – and it was not long afterwards that compressed air was applied to cutting coal. The idea of some kind of mechanical cutter was not new, and in 1761 an ingenious inventor from Newcastle-upon-Tyne had tried out a horse-driven machine; but, since information about it is scanty and it seems not to have been adopted elsewhere, it presumably failed. By 1865, however, there were compressed-air-driven cutters at work at two pits in the north, Elsecar and Bishop's Close. These were disc cutters, with an edge that consisted of pickheads which could be replaced as they were blunted. Although these early machines were tributes to their inventors' ingenuity, coal cut by them was, in fact, dearer than that won by the pick, largely because of the expense of taking the compressed air supply to the working face. It was not until electricity began to be used underground, in the 1880s, that there was any real hope of taking the sweat out of coalface work, and even then progress was slow. It still had to be loaded by hand on to wagons or on to a conveyor belt – a twentieth-century invention – and so, even in pits mechanized as far as current developments would allow, until the 1940s men with shovels took over where men with picks had stopped, and the rigours of the coalface were merely extended with the noise and dust of the cutters. In 1900 only 1.5 per cent of Britain's coal was being cut by machine. By 1925 this had risen to 20 per cent, though in two-thirds of British pits coal was still won entirely by hand. Not that mechanization necessarily made working conditions much better, as George Orwell found when he went down Crippen's pit near Wigan in 1936. Having crawled several hundred yards along passages about four feet high, and sometimes much less, he reached a working face where there was one of the larger cutters, manned by a crew of five. This was a disc cutter which had to be manhandled into position in a space less than a yard high. It was fitted with runners, not wheels, and 'even to drag the thing forward must be a frightful labour, seeing that the men have to do it practically lying down'. The coal was loaded by shovel on to a conveyor belt by two 'scufters'. Orwell judged the heat to be about 100 degrees Fahrenheit. In another pit, in Yorkshire, he saw a chain cutter – a more modern type – at work: 'The place where these men, and those loading the broken coal on to the tubs, were working was like hell. . . . As the machine works it sends forth clouds of coal dust which almost stifle one and make it impossible to see more than a few feet.' Davy lamps 'of an old-fashioned pattern' gave the only light available. And at Grimethorpe, which had been reported to him as very up to date, with machinery not available elsewhere in Britain, he found conditions at the face 'fearful beyond description'. The fillers loading the cut coal on to the belt worked in a space about a yard high: 'The effort of constantly shovelling coal over your left shoulder and flinging it a yard or two beyond, while in a kneeling position, must be very great even to men who are used to it.'

A dramatic breakthrough had to await the development in the 1940s of the Anderton shearer loader, which works rather like a grocer's bacon slicer, cutting the coal and throwing it on to a conveyor, and this was the first of the modern generation of pit machinery which has been developed and brought into use since nationalization. By 1950, 79 per cent of coal was machine-cut and the proportion was to grow steadily greater. In view of the fact that the huge weeding out of collieries since then – down to 220 by 1981, now fewer – was concentrated on the less efficient pick-and-shovel pits, perhaps the really surprising statistic is that even in 1981 three out of every hundred tons of British coal were still being hewn by men with picks.

3

TRAPPERS AND HURRIERS, PUTTERS AND BEARERS

Sarah Gooder was eight years old, a trapper in the Gawber pit near Barnsley. Her job was to sit by a trapdoor in the passage between the face and the pit bottom, which controlled the ventilation, and to open it to allow the corves of coal to be hauled through. 'It does not tire me,' she said, 'but I have to trap without a light, and I'm scared. I go at four and sometimes half past three in the morning, and come out at five and half past. I never go to sleep. Sometimes I sing when I've light, but not in the dark. I dare not sing then.'

From almost the earliest age, some kind of work could be found for a child in the pit, even if it was only to hold a candle to light its father's work. Of course, some children were taken down with their fathers and mothers simply because there was nothing else to be done with them, in the absence of a childminder at home. But work could be done by even the smallest pair of hands, and it was the view of the Reverend Richard Morton, curate of Dodworth, near Barnsley, that 'the parents get their children into the pits as soon as they think they can do anything'. Some children were said to be so young that they were carried down on their fathers' backs, dressed in their bedgowns. In South Wales, a child of any age taken down the pit was a meal ticket; William Richards of Llantrisant, Glamorgan, went down with his father in 1833 when he was four, 'because times were poor, and he was worth an extra tram'. His father was entitled to hew more coal because he had registered the need to support an extra mouth. But this was a peculiarity of South Wales; generally, children taken below were expected to earn their keep. 'No sooner,' wrote H. Herbert Jones, inspecting in North Wales in 1841, 'is a collier's son able to exert a little muscular force than he becomes an underground machine destitute of the slightest mental cultivation.'

Children's earnings were paid to the father or guardian; it was not always easy to establish exact relationships, and in any case since child labour was a mere commodity it didn't matter much. Either greed or need explained the introduction of children so young, but there was also a view that it was necessary on health grounds. James Hinscliffe, the proprietor of a pit near Halifax, gave his opinion 'as a practical man' that boys should begin at the age of seven, because if they did not begin early, 'they cannot get on at all' and were more liable to deformities. James Holmes, proprietor at Long Shaw, Northowram, agreed. 'It would be impossible for us to work our pits without the use of boys as hurriers,' he said, 'because we have no other means of getting our coals to the shafts, and if they are not taken young at it they never make colliers, for this reason: that our seams are so thin that it would be impossible for older boys to hurry without greatly punishing themselves.' He thought about nine was a reasonable age for a boy to start. But it was more common for proprietors to have no views at all on the matter. Joseph Rawson, who ran his mother's pit at Bankbottom near Halifax, didn't know how many children were employed there. They were paid by the colliers weekly he believed, 'but I do not know much about that'. He did not know whether the children had breakfast before they went into the pit or whether they took any food with them. Near Brighouse, another proprietor, George Emmet, was even more ignorant of the condition of the workpeople who kept him in comfort. He did not know what their ages were, how they were paid, what time they went to work, whether they took food with them, what their moral condition was, whether they went to church or chapel or Sunday school, or what their health was like. The indifference of the coalmasters combined with the avarice of parents to make the employment of young children possible. James Warrener, a 69-year-old collier from Oldham, looked back on over sixty years in the pits and concluded that colliers in general 'went themselves into the coal pit so early they did not know their own duties'. 'There are drunken blackguards,' he added, 'that would not mind at what ages they took them, making them draw at the bottom worse than dogs, with nothing on them but their cap and belt.'

Trapping was usually a child's first job in the pit. It was necessary to be small, like Sarah Gooder. The trapper was folded, between corves, into a hollow scraped out beside the door. When he or she heard a corf coming, a string was pulled to open the door. When the string was released, the door would fall back of its own accord, unless perhaps some coal had fallen off to obstruct it, in which case the trapper had either to clear it or get help. The traps in a room and pillar pit were the essential element of the ventilation system. Especially in a pit known to be gassy, where the safety of everyone below ground depended on the efficiency of the ventilation, it was a horrifyingly responsible job to give to a child of five or even eight. But as the passages were often only two feet high, and sometimes less, trapping was a job for the very young. Its peculiar cruelty was that – except in Cumberland, where trappers' lights were allowed – it had to be done in the dark, unless a kind-hearted collier could be persuaded to part with a candle end. Trappers were inclined to see, or hear, ghosts. John Nomington, at Mr Woolley's pit at Stalybridge in Lancashire, heard a wagon coming and someone walking at the back of it, and he called out three times, and there was no answer. Sometimes Rosa Lucas, at Mr Morris's pit at Lamberhead Green, also in Lancashire, thought she saw something – the ghost, perhaps, of her father, who had been killed in the pit. 'On one occasion,' reported Jelinger Symons, inspecting in Yorkshire for the Children's Employment Commission's 1842 report, 'as I was passing a little trapper, he begged me for a little grease from my candle. I found that the poor child had scooped out a hole in a great stone and, having obtained a wick, had manufactured a rude sort of lamp; and that he kept it going as well as he could by begging contributions of melted tallow from the candles of any Samaritan passers-by.' Symons added: 'When we consider the very trifling cost at which these little creatures might be supplied with a light ... there are few things which more strongly indicate the neglect of their comfort than the fact of their being kept in darkness – of all things the most wearisome to a young child.' He could have added that light might have helped the trappers to defeat their greatest enemy, sleep. As they had to be at their posts throughout the extremities of the working shift – Sarah Gooder's fourteen hours was relatively modest compared with a couple of generations earlier, when a twenty-hour shift was commonplace and some trappers claimed to have been at work for thirty-six hours – the enemy was never far away. John Saville, working at the Soap pit, Sheffield, fell asleep one day and a corf ran over his leg. He was frightened that if he did it again he might be crushed against the wall. He had no hollow to shelter in; he had to sit against the trap and scramble out of the way of the corves as best he could. Nor was sleep the only hazard. At Awsworth, in Derbyshire, the airways were cold, and Levi Richards remembered that when he was nine and a trapper, there were icicles as thick as his arm hanging over the doorway in winter.

Not everyone considered the trapper's lot unacceptable. The manager of a Tyneside colliery, George Johnson, pointed out that it was a relatively safe job: 'The position of the trapper is always very secure,' he said, 'and strong timber supports the roof where he is sitting. A sufficiently large place is left behind the door for him to retire to and he need never move from that place, having a cord to open and shut the door.' But then he had never been a trapper. James Warrener of Oldham had, fifty years before, and his view was that 'a child of six, or seven, or eight had better be transported than sent into a coal pit'.

Children of ten or eleven could carry on trapping if they were undersized enough, but by that age most were moving on to haulage. This, in its various forms, was said to account for three-quarters of the child and female labour in the pits. The most common method was called 'hurrying' in Yorkshire, 'drawing' in Lancashire, and 'putting' in the northeast of England and the east of Scotland. The task of the hurrier was to pull loaded corves of coal from the working face to the bottom of the pit shaft, or in larger pits to the nearest point that horses could be brought to. The way lay along the air passages, which were perhaps two feet six inches high but often less, the thickness of the seam as a rule, and through the trapdoors which tended to be a few inches smaller. It was necessary to go on all fours, pulling the corf by means of a belt round the waist from which a chain passed between the legs. In some pits the corves were wheeled and ran on tramways, but in the older and more run-down workings there were no rails, the floor was uneven and the corves had sledge runners. If a corf got stuck, as often happened even on the tramways because of poor maintenance of the tracks or the jamming of the corf wheels – or if a slope was particularly steep – the hurrier might have to unhook the chain, scramble to the back and push, using hands and head. Hurrying was hardest when the hewers were working 'to dip' – that is, when the working face was at a lower level than the passages and so the loaded corves had to be hurried uphill. Then the hurriers might work in pairs, one pulling and the other pushing, or 'thrusting' or 'thrutching' as it was called. Thrutchers provided themselves with padded caps, but these did not prevent them from bald patches and huge blisters on the crown of the head.

Hurriers generally went below an hour or two after the getters, so that there was a stock of coal for them to haul as soon as they arrived. At the other end of the shift, the getters left early and the hurriers worked on, hauling the coal that had been cut, making several more round trips between the working face and the shaft. The number of journeys each shift naturally varied with the distance to be covered, somewhere between twelve and twenty-four, but it was reckoned in Yorkshire that in a typical twelve-hour shift a hurrier might go about three and a half miles, half of which would be done pulling a total weight, allowing for the corf and its contents, of perhaps eight hundredweight, though there was no standard weight or capacity for a corf. The strain, it was noted, sometimes made hurriers bleed at the nose. At Patricroft, near Manchester, it was claimed that one girl hurrier had on one occasion travelled nearly fourteen miles in a single shift of fourteen or fifteen hours, but this was exceptional and may have been a legend.

In thick seams, the loading or filling of the corves was a separate job, but most hurriers had, between journeys, to do their own loading and, in some pits, riddling, so that in pits where there was no official meal-break in mid-shift (and that was most of them) the only time when a hurrier was not doing hard physical work was while waiting in turn at the shaft for the corf to be tallied – marked down to a particular getter. The riddle was a sieve about two feet across and three inches deep. The hurrier held it out while a shovelful of coal and slack was thrown in, shook the slack through and tipped the coal into the corf. When almost full, the corf was 'topped' with several pieces of large coal and was ready for another trip.

In some pits, notably round Halifax, there were 5- and 6-year old hurriers at work, usually in pairs with one pulling and the other thrutching. Pulling was the harder work, but thrutching the more hazardous, and it was common for thrutchers to have lost one or more fingers which had been crushed against the top or sides of the passages. By eleven or so, most hurriers were working on their own. Fanny Drake was fifteen when she was interviewed at Charlesworth's Wood pit near Wakefield in 1841. She had been hurrying for six years, she said, sometimes up to her calves in water. She remembered the whole of one winter before a pump was installed, when it had been like this, and her feet were 'skinned, and just as if they were scalded, for the water was bad'. She had also had headaches and nosebleeds and had taken time off work. Fanny did a twelve-hour shift, with a break at midday for half an hour if she was lucky and the getter she worked for, James Greenwood, had no objection. Sometimes they would take a rest together. She had done her share of thrutching: 'It makes my head sore sometimes, so that I cannot bear it touched; it is soft too.' Hurrying was 'middling hard work', she reckoned.

As a hurrier's life went, Fanny was relatively lucky. The passages where she worked were a fairly generous thirty-two inches to a yard high. Her getter treated her reasonably well. The corves at the Wood pit weighed about five hundredweight fully laden, less than many others elsewhere. At Booth Town pit, Halifax, 17-year-old Patience Kershaw ('an ignorant, filthy, ragged and deplorable-looking object', noted her interviewer, 'and such a one as the uncivilized natives of the prairies would be shocked to look upon') was less fortunate. She was one of ten fatherless children, of whom six were, or had been, hurriers. She did a twelve-hour shift, from five to five, but there was no midday break at Booth Town: 'I take my dinner with me, a cake, and eat it as I go; I do not stop or rest at any time for the purpose.' Patience hurried eleven corves a shift, working 'to dip', each trip covering more than a mile. The getters and the other hurriers treated her badly; she was the only girl in the pit, and so perhaps particularly vulnerable: 'Sometimes they beat me, if I am not quick enough, with their hands; they strike me upon the back; the boys take liberties with me sometimes, they pull me about.' Her earnings were eight-and-six a week, about a sixth of the money coming into the Kershaw household.

It was the situation of the girl hurriers that most excited the compassion of humanitarian observers. 'The estimation of the sex,' wrote one of the inspectors to the 1841 Commission, 'has ever been held a test of the civilization of a people. Shall it then be said that in the very heart of our own country – from which missions are daily sent to teach God's law, and millions upon millions have been generously poured forth for the manumission of hosts in a distant land – that there shall exist a state of society in which hundreds of young girls are sacrificed to such shameless indecencies, filthy abominations and cruel slavery as is found to exist in our coal pits? Chained, belted, harnessed, like dogs in a go-cart – black, saturated with wet, and more than half-naked – crawling upon their hands and feet, and dragging their heavy loads behind them – they present an appearance indescribably disgusting and unnatural.' A colleague who had visited South Wales agreed; he wrote of 'repulsive objects . . . degraded and almost unsexed beings I have often beheld, with mingled horror and compassion'. All this is heady stuff, and has led at least one modern historian to find it possible to sneer at the inspectors as predisposed to believe all they were told. They were, he said, deceived by 'the artistry with which young children can wring the hearts of innocent adults when they think it will suit their purpose', and too ready to take advantage of 'the sexual element in the report'. But there can be no doubt that the inspectors' expressions of horror were genuinely felt and the result not of hearsay but of the evidence of their own eyes. The story of the hurriers is a piece of history that cannot be rewritten. And as for harnessing girls 'like dogs in a go-cart', dog-carts had only narrowly missed being banned nationally by an Act of 1835, and in 1839 had been banished from a fifteen-mile radius of Charing Cross by the Metropolitan Police Act. At Whitehaven Colliery in 1801, horses were worked in relays of three hours only in order to spare them. But this was a society whose Royal Society for the Prevention of Cruelty to Animals preceded its counterpart for children by sixty years.

Fanny Drake and Patience Kershaw were typical hurriers, but there was no common standard between coalfields, or even between one pit and its neighbour, as to the age or sex of hurriers, or the way they worked, or the way they were paid. What was common, however, and this was where Fanny was lucky, was the systematic brutality by which hurriers were got to work and made to work harder. Patience was unusual in apparently working for more than one getter. The more usual practice was for the getter to contract to supply so many corves at the pit bottom, and then to hire and pay his own hurrier or, if they were young, more than one. The getter's agreement would tend to be based on how much coal he could hew rather than how much could be hurried, so that the hurrier was constantly struggling to keep up. Any delay en route, such as a corf sticking or, in railed pits, coming off the tramway – in which case it had to be lifted on again by brute force – would lead to a thrashing when the hurrier got back to the face. Pick handles and other tools, belts and boots were used fairly indiscriminately, and there was always a supply of yardsticks, the tallies put into each corf to identify the getter, which made effective implements. At Hutchby's pit in Derbyshire the men used on the boys a stick as thick as a hedge stake; one boy was beaten and knocked down, and then stamped on so that he could hardly stand. In the same pit, 14-year-old James Robinson had a stick as thick as two fingers broken over him. At Butterley Park, still in Derbyshire, Constantine Neale had his toe cut off at work, but he was made to work on to the end of the shift. He was off work for four months afterwards. The younger and weaker hurriers were also at the mercy of the older ones when it came to waiting turn to unload at the shaft. The older ones would fight for a better place, and this meant delay and yet more trouble from the getter. Esther Craven started hurrying in the Clewes Moor pit near Halifax when she was nine, and at eight her sister Harriet joined her as a thrutcher. They worked for a collier named Joseph Ibbotson, a famous bully. On the day that the government inspector interviewed them in 1841, he found Harriet crying bitterly because Ibbotson had just hit her in the back with a piece of coal as big as her head. 'Both herself and her sister,' the inspector noted, 'informed me that he was constantly in the habit of ill-treating them; the several marks upon their persons which they showed me were sufficient proofs of it.' Samuel Walkden, a collier all his life at the Low Side pit near Oldham, thought nothing of it. 'The children, when bedtime comes on them, begin to be drowsy and sleepy in the night,' he said, 'and the only way to keep them awake is to give them a good sowse on the side of the head, kick their arses, or give them a good shake.' At Low Side, the night shift sometimes worked through Saturday night, 'cheating the Lord as they thought', becoming the day shift on Monday morning for the following week.

It was better, on the whole, to hurry for a getter who was not a relative, because arrangements were then on a proper business footing and the hurrier had some negotiating power over wages; though there were disadvantages in this for girl hurriers, as some getters were not beyond enlivening the midday break with a bout of sex. If you hurried for your father, or your elder brother, or your uncle, you might never see your earnings, or know what they were, or get any benefit from them. Thirteen-year-old John Harvey was a hurrier – they called them 'carters' there – at the Crown pit, Warmley, in south Gloucestershire: 'A pitiable specimen,' it was reported, 'of a much enduring class of colliery boys, whose subsistence depends on their own exertions, often prematurely stimulated, either from being deprived of their father's by death, or labouring under the curse of drunken, dissolute and unfeeling parents, who would apathetically see their children enslave themselves rather than contribute to their comfort by a single act of self-denial.' John's father, though in work, was a drunkard and his mother a slut. John reckoned himself lucky to get any kind of meal when he got home from work; it might be potatoes and butter or, on a very good day, potatoes fried with bacon. But he had sometimes gone without food for two or three days. He had no clothes except what he worked in, and had never had a pair of shoes or stockings in his life. He earned sixpence a day and sometimes worked through the night for an extra sixpence; not that he ever saw any of it.

Worst off of all were the poorhouse children who were apprenticed to the pits, usually at about eight or nine (the official age for poor-law apprentices was nine) but sometimes as young as four or five. Apprenticeships lasted for twelve years, during which period the boys were paid perhaps sixpence a week pocket money for working alongside hurriers or getters who were paid the full rate for the job, and often forced to go where other boys would not. Pit apprenticeships were widespread in the eighteenth century, but by the mid-nineteenth were confined to south Staffordshire, Yorkshire, Lancashire and, to a lesser extent, the west of Scotland.

This is what apprenticeship was like for Thomas Moorhouse, who was bound when he was nine to a collier named William Greenwood: 'He was bound to find me in victuals and drink and clothes; I never had enough; I used to have porridge and treacle water, and sometimes dry cake and coffee; he gave me some old clothes to wear which he bought at the rag shop; the overseers gave him a sovereign to buy clothes but he never laid it out.' Thomas slept three in a chaff bed with his master's son and nephew. 'We used to lie top o' the tick without anything else, and had an old blanket and ragged sheet to cover us.' He went to bed at eight or nine, got up at five in the morning and had breakfast, taking a dry cake to work with him, but nothing to drink. Greenwood hit him frequently with anything that came to hand – the boy was found to have more than twenty scars, including one from being hit with a pickhead – and Thomas finally ran away: ' . . . and went about to see if I could get a job. I used to sleep in the cabins on the pit's bank, and in the old pits that had done working. I used to get what I could to eat; I ate for a long time the candles that I found in the pits that the colliers had left overnight.' He was lucky in that Greenwood had lost his indentures and so could not go to the justices for an order to bring him back. Eventually, after a period of begging, he found a month's work near Bradford, replacing a hurrier who was sick, and then became a hurrier for a collier who treated him well.

Edmund Kershaw, of Castleton in Lancashire, was another victim of the apprenticeship system. His mother, a widow, was unable to keep him, and he was bound by the parish overseers to a collier named Robert Brierley at Balsgate. He was employed as a wagoner until, starved and beaten and with a fractured arm for which he had received no attention over several weeks, Brierley sent him home in a cart as of no further use. His mother complained to the overseers; the boy was unable to sit or stand, and was placed on the floor of the office, laid on his side on a small cradle bed. It was discovered that he had been systematically beaten about the head and body with a piece of wood through which half an inch of nail projected, and had been forced to continue working after he had fractured his arm in an accident. Near Blackburn, Roger Taylor was apprenticed to the Bank Moor Colliery, but after nine months the overseers called him back and the doctor pronounced that he had been so badly beaten that he was unfit for work. After some time the doctor got him fit again, and he was again sent out; this time, smallpox lay in wait, from which he died.

The use of apprentices was a particular scandal in south Staffordshire, where, it was said, 'such is the demand for children . . . that there are almost no boys in the union workhouses at Walsall, Wolverhampton, Dudley and Stourbridge'. The collieries in Bilston alone were said to have up to 300 apprentices at work. It was an arrangement which suited the parish overseers, because it took the boys off the poor rate; suited the butties or subcontractors, providing them with free labour for twelve years; suited the coalmasters, because coal hurried or got by slave labour was cheap coal; and suited the landowners because cheap coal provided a larger royalty. 'Hence all parties are interested,' the government inspector noted, 'and the pauper children suffer.' Observing that it was consistently claimed by the workhouse overseers and the masters that the apprentices were well treated and well fed, the inspector, Dr Joseph Mitchell, remarked that 'all this, and more than this, was said by the planters respecting the slaves in the West Indies; but still the country would not be satisfied, and put an end to slavery in the colonies. Now here is a slavery in the middle of England as reprehensible as ever was the slavery in the West Indies, which justice and humanity alike demand should not longer be endured.'

By the 1840s, however, Staffordshire pits were on the side of the angels in one respect: they did not employ girls or women underground. In Yorkshire, parts of Lancashire and South Wales, females were still employed underground in large numbers in the 1840s, though in other areas such as Cumberland and Durham, where women colliers were common in the eighteenth century, the practice had died out. Women were traditionally employed in haulage, though there was, in the eighteenth century, a Lancashire pit where one seam, called 'the woman's coal', was entirely worked by females. By the nineteenth, as we have seen, there was work at the bank for women, who were also employed in the ancillary trades; one observer wrote of the survival of 'a few amazons [who] yet practise the vocation of coal carriers, on their own account, from the pits into the city or suburbs, rivalling the men in strength of sinew and vigour of lungs'. Even in the areas where girls or women still worked below, there were districts, or single pits, where only men and boys were allowed underground. A collier who moved a distance of twenty-five miles in the 1820s, from Wigan – where women were still employed on the pit banks in the 1920s – to Oldham, was surprised to find only males in the pits. An Oldham collier had a story about a pit where a lone woman had been employed – this would be about 1800 – and the men had said that if she didn't leave work, they would, 'and so both she and her husband had to go'. They were paid fourteen shillings out of the benefit club to get out of the district. At the Banknock Colliery near Falkirk, in the middle of an area notorious for the hellish conditions under which the female workforce toiled, the owners allowed only men and boys to go below. There seems to have been no other reason for this kind of distinction than local custom and prejudice, or occasionally the prejudice of the landowner. Some coalmasters asserted that girls made better hurriers than boys because they were quicker and larked about less, but among the colliers themselves the reason for preferring girls was that, as very few became or wanted to become getters, they were not a threat to the men's livelihood. Peter Gaskell, a getter at Worsley, one of the Duke of Bridgewater's Lancashire pits, preferred girl hurriers because 'they are better to manage, and keep the time better; they will fight and shriek and do everything but let anybody pass them; and they never get to be coal-getters, that is another good thing.'

The worst area for underground female labour in any terms – the proportion employed, the severity of the work, and the persistence of the custom – was the east of Scotland. Here, the haulage of coal between getter and shaft, and sometimes between getter and the surface, was almost exclusively a female occupation. Boys became getters at the incredibly early age of nine or ten, or, as one collier pithily put it, as soon as they could hold a pick. Consequently the proportion of girls and women in most pits was high. It was an old Scottish tradition. Of the workforce of a colliery at Bo'ness in 1681 totalling fifty, thirty-one were women, all bearers, an occupation which is about to be examined. At Dunmore Colliery in 1769 there were fifty-seven women to forty-five men. In typical nineteenth-century Scottish collieries the proportions had reversed, but the employment of females was still significant: at the Duke of Hamilton's Redding pit in Stirlingshire, 127 of the 447-strong workforce were women or girls; at the Alloa Coal Company's pit, 100 out of 349; and at the Carron pit at Falkirk, 137 out of 345.

There were two methods of haulage in the pits of the east of Scotland: 'putting', the Scottish name for hurrying, using the 'slype', the local version of the corf which was an iron-keeled wooden box holding between two and five hundredweight, and 'bearing', carrying the coal on the back in a creel basket. The slype was the usual method in Mid- and East Lothian, and though the harness by which it was drawn was less physically disgusting than the belt and chain of the English coalfields – the Lothian version went over the shoulders and round the waist, with the drawing thong fastened to the back of the belt and passing over the back of the legs instead of between them – the work itself was harder, aided by neither wheels nor even runners. 'It is almost incredible,' reported Robert Franks, a government inspector, after seeing the slype in use, 'that human beings can submit to such employment, crawling on hands and knees, harnessed like horses, over soft, slushy floors more difficult than dragging the same weights through our lowest common sewers, and more difficult in consequence of the inclination, which is frequently one in three to one in six.' The evidence of many of the Scottish girls, however, made it all too clear how they could submit to such employment. 'Father makes me like it' was a frequent comment. 'I don't like the work,' said 15-year-old Margaret Drysdale, 'but mother is dead and father brought me down; I had no choice.' Twelve-year-old Catherine Meiklejohn did a thirteen-hour shift; she 'would not like to work so long, only father bids me'. Jane Kerr, twelve, was among the many girls whose fathers kept them going with the strap.

Putting the slype was, as Katherine Logan, who was sixteen and had been doing it for five years, said, 'o'er sair work'. But it was not as savagely oppressive as coal bearing. This, literally climbing out of the pit with coals on your back, was a peculiarity of pits where the seams ran vertically or near vertically. In Scotland these were called 'edge seams'. It was perfectly possible, and indeed it was practised in South Wales, to exploit vertical seams without using women and children as beasts of burden. The method involved making a series of inclines down which skips or tubs were run, controlled by a windlass at the top. For those who guided the skips down, or hauled them up, it was tricky work and physically tiring, but not savagely brutal. But in Scotland edge seams were worked by building a winding staircase, spiral fashion, from the workings to the surface, or by arranging a series of ladders. It is hard to believe that even in the 1840s, when the working classes were regarded as lower than the animals, it could have been possible for human beings to have been worked as the coal bearers of the Lothians were.

Alison Jack was eleven and worked at the Loanhead Colliery near Edinburgh. In 1841 she had been bearing for her father for three years. She went down with him at two in the morning and worked through till one or two in the afternoon. Her task was to carry about a ton of coal per shift. Robert Franks, the government inspector, watched Alison at work: 'She takes her creel (a basket formed to the back, not unlike a cockleshell flattened towards the neck, so as to allow lumps of coal to rest on the back of the neck and shoulders), and pursues her journey to the wall face, or as it is called here, the room of work. She then lays down her basket, into which the coal is rolled, and it is frequently more than one man can do to lift the burden on her back. The tugs or straps are placed over the forehead, and the body bent in a semicircular form, in order to stiffen the arch. Large lumps of coal are then placed on the neck, and she then commences her journey with her burden, first hanging her lamp to the cloth crossing her head.' A variant on the lighting arrangements used in some pits was for the bearer to hold a candle holder in her teeth. Alison staggered about thirty yards from the face to an eighteen-foot ladder, climbed this, went along a passage, up another eighteen-foot ladder, along another passage, up more ladders, and so on until she had carried her creel to the point reached by the shaft, where she unloaded it into a skip. Alison reckoned to do her stint in twenty journeys; if she flagged, her father was handy with the strap. Robert Franks found that girls as young as six were doing this work, carrying half-hundredweight loads, progressing as they grew older to about a hundredweight at ten (Alison's load, between one and one and a half hundredweight, was thought to be about right for her age) to two hundredweight at sixteen and three or more in adulthood. 'I have,' reported Franks, 'taken the evidence of fathers who have ruptured themselves from straining to lift coal on their children's backs.' At Haugh Lynn Colliery, Midlothian, 10-year-old Mary Neilson ('If well dressed would vie with any child in Scotland in point of beauty,' noted Franks) made ten to fifteen 'rakes' (journeys) a day usually, but when her sister was away she had to do twenty. Her load was one hundredweight, 'and it is no easy work'. She had been bearing since she was six. Sixteen-year-old Mary Duncan claimed to carry two hundredweight. 'Some females carry two and a half to three,' she added, 'but it is overstraining.' 'I am very glad,' said Alison Jack, 'when my task is wrought, as it sore fatigues.' 'Coal bearing is horrible sore work,' Margaret Jacques, a 17-year-old bearer, said. 'It was not my choice, but we do our parents' will.'

'It is revolting to humanity to reflect upon the barbarous and cruel slavery which this degrading labour constitutes,' wrote Franks. 'It is the remnant of the slavery of a degraded age.' He was not the first to protest publicly at the particular horror of bearing. In 1793, Lord Dundonald banned the employment of women as carriers in his own pits and began a campaign to enlighten other coalowners. In 1808 an Edinburgh coalmaster described bearing as 'severe, slavish and oppressive in the highest degree', rendering the bearers' existence 'the most weary of all the pilgrimages of this journey through life'. It was dangerous as well as exhausting. The bearers followed one another closely up ladder or stair, exposed to falling lumps of coal or indeed a whole load, often having to keep close together to share the light from the leader's candle. Sometimes the strap round the bearer's head would break, and both load and bearer would fall from the ladder. Margaret NcNeil of Edmonstone Colliery in Midlothian was fairly lucky when this happened to her; she escaped with two broken legs. A further danger arose in some Scottish pits because bearers and putters had to do their own unloading into the shaft corves at the pit bottom. At Edmonstone, 16-year-old Helen Reid had a narrow escape when she was unloading and the corf unexpectedly began to rise: 'The hook caught me by my pit clothes. The people did not hear my shrieks. My hand had fast grappled the chain, and the great height of the shaft caused me to lose my courage, and I swooned. The banksman [at the top of the shaft] could scarcely remove my hand. The deadly grasp saved my life.' Helen Bowman of Dundonald Colliery in Fife, who was about to be married, was less lucky; the hook caught her clothes and she was carried up, falling from near the top of the shaft. It took her two days to die.

Managers and owners in Scotland, with one or two exceptions, found themselves well able to face the accident rates in their pits with equanimity, as indeed they did the atrocious conditions of work and the tender age and sex of many of those who performed it. The proprietor of Bo'ness Colliery in Linlithgowshire, James Cadell, had a robust attitude on the question of age: 'I think the parents are the best judges when to take their children below for assistance,' he said. (Mr Cadell's was the pit where Robert Sneddon was killed by a roof fall. 'No one came to inquire about how he was killed,' reported his sister Mary. 'They never do in this place.') It was often claimed by the parents of the underground children that, much as they regretted the necessity to send them down, their families could not survive without the extra earnings, and many coalmasters supported this argument with crocodile tears. 'We are beset by the entreaties of fathers and of widows to employ their young children,' said one, 'and are in a manner compelled to do it.' Any attempt to legislate against the employment of young children, said another, would be resented by the colliers, 'who would consider such interference anything but an act of humanity displayed towards them'. No doubt there were some families in real difficulties, such as that of Rachel Tinker of Hepworth in Yorkshire, who was one of six daughters her father had put to hurrying because, she explained, 'We have no boys and we would be fast if he couldn't send us to the pit.' But it was noticeable, particularly in the east of Scotland, how many children whose entire families, including their mothers, were working below were supporting a father who was said to be off work with 'bad breath' or some similarly vague complaint. Jane Kerr and Emma Bennett, two 12-year-old bearers, both noted that their fathers didn't work on Mondays, and sometimes not on Tuesdays, though both girls had to go down as usual. Robert Franks perhaps discovered the reason for the frequent indisposition of fathers when he investigated the number of licensed houses in the pit towns and villages. Clackmannan was top of the league with a licensed house for every seventy-two inhabitants; the more usual proportion was one to 100. (But there was no settlement in Scotland to approach the record set up by a South Wales pit hamlet, Tongwinlais in the Vale of Taff, where there was one licensed house for every twenty-eight villagers.)

In Scotland and elsewhere, some owners and managers expressly forbade the employment of the youngest children, though even if they made rules these were not always adequately supervised, and managements were often too removed from the actual operations of the pit to notice. In many cases the eyes of managers tended to cloud over if the question of age was raised by the government inspectors, and it seemed as if they, their parents and others were engaged in some conspiracy to get the children below as soon as possible. Workhouse authorities joined in this with a will, and since the registration of births and deaths did not become compulsory until 1836 it was not possible until 1845 to check whether, for example, apprentices were being bound younger than at the permitted age of nine. In 1840, a collier from the Thornhill pit in Yorkshire went to Batley workhouse and took on trial a boy named Thomas Townsend, just four years old. Within three weeks, Thomas was back at Batley, some said because he was caught thieving at a neighbour's house, others because his grandfather had heard about it and objected to his being bound apprentice so young. 'He was entered in my book as being born in 1836,' said Mrs Lee, the Batley workhouse matron, adding lamely, 'I believe there was a mistake made by the board about his age.' But they were hazy about ages and obligations at Batley workhouse. There was another incident the previous year when a 7-year-old boy, Joseph Booth, was, despite the objections of a board member who was a surgeon, bound apprentice to Robert Lumb, a collier who had obtained five or six other young children in the same way. After nine months, the boy was returned because Lumb had not found him strong enough – or rather, that was one version of the story. Mrs Lee had a different tale: Joseph's uncle had taken him away from Lumb, she said, because he was not getting enough to eat.

There was, for the boys at least, a recognizable career path, if one could call it that, underground. They had some hope of one day, by say eighteen or twenty, becoming getters on their own account (which is to say, seeing the colour of their own earnings, unless they were apprentices), and so achieving some independence; and indeed nineteen or twenty was the usual age of marriage for a young collier, though in Glamorgan it was said to be rather younger – seventeen or eighteen was the average round about 1840, and fourteen or fifteen was not uncommon. (Until 1929, males in England could marry at fourteen and females at twelve.) James Pearce of Lawley in Shropshire had a typical early career. He went down the pit when he was seven, trapping for sixpence a day, and after about eighteen months he went 'to walk with a candle before the horses, and pick the coals off the road' for eightpence. Then he took to the girdle and chain, drawing unwheeled skips on unrailed roads, earning eighteenpence a day which rose to twenty-eight. He thought that 'if I kept drawing I should be nothing at all', so he took a cut in wages to twelve shillings a week and went to drive horses on the bank. Then he went below again, filling the skips for three shillings a day. If he stayed in the pit, and it was certain that, barring death or injury, he would, he could expect to earn twenty-five shillings a week when he was eighteen, and after that there would be little improvement. But at least the solitude of trapping and the agony of drawing with the belt and chain led somewhere. Though women getters were not unknown in some places, in most areas haulage with the corf or creel was as far as a female could progress. She might exchange hurrying for her father to hurrying for her husband, but she would remain subordinate all her working life. A woman could carry on as a drawer in Lancashire or as a putter or bearer in the east of Scotland as long as she cared, or as long as her health or child-bearing permitted. At thirty-seven, Betty Harris of Little Bolton in Lancashire could look back on a lifetime of drawing with the belt and chain. Because of the steep slopes in her pit there were ropes along the way to help the drawers along. Little Bolton was a wet pit, and Betty worked with water always over the tops of her clogs, 'and I have seen it up to my thighs'. She worked all day in clothes wet through, going home to fall asleep often before she had washed. 'I have drawn till I have had the skin off me,' she said. She drew for the man she lived with, who 'has beaten me many a time for not being ready'. The belt and chain, she said, were worse when women were in the family way.

Being in the family way meant harder work while a woman stayed below and potentially a disastrous loss of earnings after the birth unless she could find a minder. Even if she could, there was the added discomfort, when she went back to work, of her milk. Most women stayed at work until the last possible moment, and miscarriages and stillbirths were frequent. Isabel Wilson, a 38-year-old mother of seven who was a putter at Elphingston Colliery in East Lothian, had been putting since she was eight. In addition to her seven living children, looked after when she was in the pit by a girl of ten, she had had three stillbirths and five miscarriages 'from the strains'. At the same pit, Margaret Reid 'came on' as she was going down in the basket. She just had time to scramble out at the pit bottom and bore her child beside the shaft. Betty Wardle of Outwood in Lancashire also had a child born in the pit, and brought it up the shaft in her skirt. She remembered it particularly because 'it was born the day after I were married, that makes me to know'. Elizabeth McNeil of Elphingston knew a woman who 'came up and the child was born in the field next the coal hill'. 'Women frequently miscarry below and suffer much after,' she added. 'Vast numbers of women are confined before they have time to change themsel'.'

But it was not the births or stillbirths that concerned the inspectors of 1841 so much as the conceptions or the possibility of conceptions. They were greatly affected by the moral risks run underground by the girls, and were shocked to find themselves moving in circles where brides were customarily pregnant, if they had not already given birth; where a man who was prudent enough to be allowed to choose his own wife would choose one more often for her strength than for her looks or domestic accomplishments; and where a collier could remark casually, with no sense of making a confession, that he habitually had sex with the girls who hurried for him and had had several children by them. It is not altogether easy to understand the inspectors' reactions to all this, at a time when bastardy was commonplace everywhere, the streets of every city teeming with prostitutes, Newcastle alone was said to contain over 100 brothels, and pregnant brides were as often seen in the country as in pit villages. Among the reasons why an 11 year-old girl should not be made to climb up four ladders and clamber, bent nearly double, along passages three feet in height with over a hundredweight of coal on her back, the fact that she might be trained up in the ways of vice seems, to modern eyes, to rank fairly low in importance.

The greatest worry for the inspectors was in those areas where girls hurried for getters to whom they were not related, though there was a girl in Yorkshire who hurried for her father-in-law and who, 'having been attempted to be ravished frequently by him', could not be got down into the pit again. It was certainly true that the bearers most to be pitied in the east of Scotland, though not necessarily for moral reasons, were the 'fremd' or 'fremit bearers' (Ger. *fremd* = strange, foreign) who were unattatched to a collier's family and were hired on a casual basis. 'These unfortunates,' says one commentary, 'had not even the protection which the self-interest of the slave owner ensures to the slave, for they were transferred from one hewer to another and might find themselves in the service of a new master each day.' Their misfortune, however, seemed more likely to be in the way of hard work and brutal treatment than moral danger, and Scottish workings give the impression of being heavily populated. The grave danger, as the inspectors saw it, was in the system whereby 'the girls go constantly, when hurrying, to the men, who work often alone in the bank faces apart from everyone'. Flockton pit in Yorkshire, for example, had a high reputation for bastardy. 'In some pits,' reported a 'respectable inhabitant, a female', who, as is often the way with such informants, was not prepared to be identified by name, 'scenes pass which are as bad as any house of ill fame'; though she did not indicate how she came to be able to make such a comparison. The Reverend Oliver

Collins, rector of Ossett near Wakefield, reported that 'bastardy is sadly too common; they look on it as a misfortune, and not as a crime.' 'Women brought up in this way,' opined a magistrate, 'lay aside all modesty, and scarcely know what it is but by name.'

The serious moral injury to which pitgirls were exposed arose largely from the fact that most getters worked naked – though some wore a shirt and waistcoat – while many hurriers, girls as well as boys, worked stripped to the waist. 'On descending Messrs Hopwood's pit at Barnsley,' reported Jelinger Symons, the inspector for Yorkshire, 'I found assembled round the fire a group of men, boys and girls, some of whom were of the age of puberty, the girls as well as the boys stark naked down to the waist, their hair bound up with a tight cap, and trousers supported by their hips. Their sex was recognizable only by their breasts, and some little difficulty occasionally arose in pointing out to me which were girls and which were boys, and which caused a good deal of laughing and joking.' But it was hard to get at the truth. Five of the girls round the fire were interviewed that evening, out of the pit, and turned up well dressed and modest. Elizabeth Day, seventeen and a hurrier, gave a clear and frank account of herself: she went to the pit when she was eight, trapped for two years and then hurried; hurried for her father, at first with her sister but latterly on her own; hurried in trousers, usually stripped to the waist but, 'I had my shift on today when I saw you, because I had had to wait, and was cold.' It was hard work for them all, but the men treated the girls well and never insulted them. Ann Mallender, fifteen, had been at the pit for six years, trapping for three and hurrying since. Between hurrying, she riddled and helped to fill. They used her pretty well at the pit. Ann's sister Betty was also started when she was nine, and dressed the same way, in trousers but stripped to the waist. She 'didn't like being in the pit, but I'm forced', but 'they never abuse me nor hit me'. Bessy Bailey was just coming up to fifteen. She liked it well enough in the pit, hurrying with her brother. She dressed like the others, naked to the waist with trousers below. So did Mary Day, sixteen, though she sometimes wore her shift. She riddled and helped to fill, as well as hurrying. She had never heard bad language or swearing in the pit. The five of them had clearly been coached; they could not deny what Jelinger Symons had seen for himself, but there were glosses that could be, and artfully had been, put in their mouths.

Other evidence was discouraging. 'At Silkstone there are a great many girls who work in the pits,' reported Barnsley solicitor Edward Newman, 'and I have seen them washing themselves naked much below the waist as I passed their doors, and whilst they are doing this they will be talking and chatting with any men who happen to be there with the utmost unconcern; and men, young and old, would be washing in the same place at the same time.' 'In my belief sexual intercourse does take place,' said Matthew Fountain, an understeward at Darton Colliery in the West Riding, 'owing to the opportunities, and owing to lads and girls working together, and owing to some of the men working in banks apart, and having girls coming to them to fill the corves, and being alone together. The girls hurry for other men than their relations, and generally prefer it.'

Understandably, though perhaps not for the most important reasons, it was belt-and-chain work that aroused the greatest horror among Mr Symons and his colleagues, especially when it was done by girls. Mr Symons went so far as to say that, given corves of reasonable weight – say up to eight hundredweight – and well maintained, running on tramways kept in good shape, 'the mere labour of hurrying is by no means great; not greater than a healthy child of thirteen (or of nine with another, where the corves are heavy) may easily perform.' An eight-hour shift, with a half-hour break at midday, was reasonable, he reckoned – but 'the foregoing remarks . . . apply to males only'.

'One of the most disgusting sights I have ever seen,' he went on, 'was that of young females, dressed like boys in trousers, crawling on all fours, with belts round their waists, and chains passing between their legs. . . . In one [pit], near New Mills, the chain, passing high up between the legs of two of these girls, had worn large holes in their trousers, and any sight more disgustingly indecent or revolting can scarcely be imagined than these girls at work. No brothel can beat it.' Interviewed later, one of the girls, Mary Holmes, who was fourteen, denied that her trousers ever got torn. She liked being in the pit and didn't want to do anything else. The work didn't make her legs or back ache. 'I am sure nobody has told me what to say,' she added disarmingly, but Mr Symons was not deceived. She was 'evidently crammed with her evidence', he noted, and he was supported in this by Ebenezer Healey, a 13-year-old who hurried in the same pit, and who told him that the girls' trousers were torn many a time, 'and when they are going along we can see them all between the legs naked; I have often; and that girl, Mary Holmes, was so today; she denies it, but it is true for all that.' Occasionally, there were attempts to dispose of unsightly evidence. Samuel Scriven, at Elland, near Halifax, interviewed a hurrier named Susan Pitchforth. 'She stood shivering before me from cold. The rag that hung about her waist was once called a shift, which is as black as the coal she thrusts, and saturated with water, the drippings of the roof and shaft. During my examination of her the banksman whom I had left in the pit came to the public house and wanted to take her away because, as he expressed himself, it was not decent that she should be (her person) exposed to us. Oh, no! It was criminal above ground; and, like the two or three other colliers in the cabin, he became evidently mortified that these deeds of darkness should be brought to light.'

Not everyone, however, feared for the morals of girls working in these conditions. Henry Briggs, a partner in the Overton pit near Wakefield, thought pitgirls made good wives. 'When they become wives and mothers of families,' he said, 'they are more clean than girls who don't go to pits, perhaps, because they are so dirty that they are forced to wash themselves well when they come out in the evening. I am decidedly of opinion that they are more cleanly and less immoral than girls who work in factories. They will know as much, if not more, of household duties than factory girls.' In fact, Mr Briggs was pretty well pleased with things all round, and painted an attractive picture of life in the pit and its village, with its good cottages with little bits of garden, allotments for potatoes, with ample schools which put on evening activities such as singing classes. But if children were kept out of the pits, his own – which produced the best coal in Yorkshire, he said – would have to close. It would be too costly to heighten the under-ground roadways so that draught animals rather than draught children could be employed. This was the kind of argument with which industrial reformers were to become depressingly familiar over the next century and, indeed, down to our own day. The price of matches would become prohibitive unless the match girls of east London continued to rot their jaws away by using phosphorus. Industry would be severely damaged and factories might have to close down if the school-leaving age were raised. Thousands might be thrown out of work if the use of asbestos were banned, for all that hundreds would waste away to a lingering death if it were not.

Conditions in the coalfields were fairly well down the list when, from the beginning of the nineteenth century onwards, humanitarians began to take an interest in how the working class worked and lived. The superficial reason for this, cited by, among others, John and Barbara Hammond, and faithfully relayed by others, was that those with interests in coal 'included men of great power and influence, men like Lord Londonderry, Lord Durham, Lord Melbourne, Lord Granville. These noblemen did not wash their hands of the business that made their wealth, for they took an active part in putting down strikes and crushing trade unions.' It is true enough that Lord Londonderry was capable of using a sledge hammer to crack a strike, as when he threatened to destroy a whole community, port, traders and all, unless his colliers went back to work; and that Lord Melbourne resisted the repeal of the anti-union Combination Acts. But many of those who came eventually to support the abolition of child and female labour in the pits, better safety standards and other reforms – including, of course, Lord Ashley – were equally opposed to trade unions; while the substantial House of Lords interest in rents from land on which the factories of Lancashire were built did not prevent successes in the campaign to improve conditions there, beginning with the Health and Morals of Apprentices Act of 1802 and followed by a number of measures culminating in the Factory Act of 1833. It was after this that Ashley (who was to become Lord Shaftesbury in 1851, when his father died) began to take an interest in the pits, and it was due to his influence that a Children's Employment Commission was set up in October 1840 on a permanent basis, taking mines as their priority. A more likely answer to the question of why it should have taken so long to investigate the coal industry is simply that it was carried on in remote areas which were cut off socially and administratively from the outside world. To contemplate the dangers and distress which went into digging out of the ground a commodity so familiar from everyday domestic use required an effort of the imagination which was simply not available in the early nineteenth century. At the same time, the coal industry lacked the occasional humanitarians such as John Fielden and John Bright who championed the cause of textile workers.

The Commissioners on the Employment of Children set about

their task with a speed that present-day official inquiries might emulate. With their brief extended in the spring of 1841 to include 'young persons' (from thirteen to eighteen), and having concerned themselves extracurricularly with the wider topic of female employment underground, they were able to report in April 1842 in three hefty volumes totalling some 2500 closely printed fools-cap pages, including evidence from several thousand witnesses. They spoke to working colliers and their families, but also to general practitioners, workhouse overseers, solicitors, coalowners, teachers, parish clerks, and indeed to almost anyone who might have anything useful to say. Unusually for a Stationery Office publication of the time, the report was illustrated, mainly to show the labour of hurrying and putting, trapping and bearing, and it was possibly these drawings that produced the report's greatest impact. But, although in the main body of the report the Commissioners were scathing about conditions underground and the attitudes of the coalowners, their final conclusions were surprisingly muted. For example, they considered that hurrying, 'so far from being in itself an unhealthy employment, is a description of exercise which, while it greatly develops the muscles of the arms, shoulders, chest, back and legs, without confining any part of the body in an unnatural and constrained posture, might, but for the abuse of it, afford an equally healthy excitement to all the other organs'. It is difficult to see how this description could be applied to the task of spending twelve or more hours a day on hands and knees dragging several hundredweights of coal along a narrow tunnel with the belt and chain, but for all its reticence when it came to recommendations the report galvanized Peel's government to such effect that a Mines Bill, prohibiting the employment underground of all girls and women, and of boys under ten, was enacted by the year's end.

In common with much early reforming legislation, however, the Mines Act of 1842 lacked teeth. It contained no reference to inspection or to penalties. Engels may have been overstating the case when he complained in 1844 that the Act 'remained a dead letter in most districts', or perhaps he was expecting too much too soon; but certainly it was reported in 1843 that there were more than sixty women still at work underground in the Duke of Hamilton's Scottish pits, and in 1844 the *Manchester Guardian* reported the death of a girl in a pit explosion near Wigan. In any case, the removal of women, girls and boys under ten was only the start of necessary reform; at any age, the belt and chain was a gross affront to human dignity. In 1860, the minimum age for underground work was raised to twelve, but six years later the Labour movement pioneer Tom Mann started work at the Victoria Colliery at Foleshill in Warwickshire. He was just ten. His account of the work is depressingly similar to those collected by the Commissioners twenty-five years before. His job was to keep the air courses clear, hauling away muck hewn out by men heading a new road or mending an old one. 'For this removal,' he remembered in his sixties, 'there were boxes known down the mine as "dans", about two feet six inches long and eighteen inches wide and of a similar depth, with an iron ring strongly fixed at each end. I had to draw the box along, not on rails; it was built sledgelike, and each boy had a belt and chain. A piece of stout material was fitted on the boy round the waist. To this there was a chain attached, and the boy would hook the chain to the box and, crawling on all fours, the chain between his legs, would drag the box along. . . . Many a time did I lie down groaning as a consequence of the heavy strain on the loins, especially when the road was wet and "clayey", causing much resistance to the load being dragged. . . . Donkey work it certainly was.'

But in one coalfield at least – in the thin seams of the north Somerset district – the belt and chain (or 'guss and crook' as it was known locally) was to serve for many more years. When, largely as a result of the interest of the fearsome Lady Astor, a Home Office Committee was set up in 1927 to investigate the matter, there was the usual weary parade of arguments for the retention of draught human labour, familiar from the report of the Children's Employment Commission almost a century earlier. To abandon the guss and crook would mean the closure of pits. The carting boys in fact learnt how to use the device very quickly. The men would see any attempt to interfere with its use as an intrusion. It was a bit hard at first, but the boys soon got used to it. The Committee's report was inconclusive, though in fact the use of the guss and crook died out during the 1930s except at one pit, where it survived until 1949.

4

'THE SAVAGE TRIBES'

They lived, some said, like pigs. Their condition, said one observer of the colliers of the West Riding, 'would be a disgrace to the savage tribes of the most savage nation, for they have at least their gods in some shape', but then he was badly affected by having spoken to a 13-year-old who did not know what was meant by 'God' or 'the Scriptures' and had never heard of Adam or Jesus Christ. (Another investigator, delighted at first to find that a child recognized the name of Christ, was dashed to discover that this was because men were frequently heard to call upon Him in the pit.) In the Lothians, it was said, colliers' homes presented 'a deplorable picture of filth and poverty' – as they continued to do until well into the present century, according to a writer who, in 1915, quoted several examples of 'the deplorable character of the housing accommodation provided by some of the companies for their miners in Scotland'. In the village of Blackwood, Monmouthshire, where there was a population of 1500, there were said, in the 1840s, to be not more than ten privies. There was a shortage of privies in Wigan too, but a poor-law official reckoned that 'such are the habits of the people that I believe if they were next door they would not go'. PC Matthew Lowe, of Wigan, also had a poor view of colliers: 'They are low, dirty, and profligate in their habits,' he said. 'Numbers have pawned every article of furniture they had.' Joseph Fletcher, inspecting in the Oldham area for the Children's Employment Commission, found little comfort in reports that the colliers of that generation were less depraved than their forebears. 'The colliery workers,' he wrote, 'are, in manners and habits, the rudest portion of a dense population proverbially rude and ignorant.'

In Scotland, a typical 'wretched hovel', perhaps ten or twelve feet square, might house up to ten people. With luck, there might be two beds for them to share, but there was often only one with, in the better-regulated homes, a curtain to divide the sexes or to separate parents from children. The rest of the furniture would consist of a few stools and maybe the odd chair, this lack of chattels being an advantage, one collier's wife explained, if the family found it necessary to flit. The family might share its home with fowls, sometimes a pig or donkey, dogs, and whatever other animals it might have, though the rules of some collieries prohibited the keeping of animals in company houses. Larks and linnets were popular cage birds; their cages were often hung in the windows, presumably to encourage them to sing but doing nothing to improve the natural light inside. Outside the door would be a pile of dung, and often 'even this filth itself is not neglected as a source of profit'. Collected from the fields, a suitable job for the youngest children, it helped pay for the whisky, explained one witness. This was in the 1840s, but there had been no great improvement by 1911, when the County Medical Officer for Dumbartonshire described the typical miner's cottage as a 'room and kitchen', one storey high in the Scottish fashion, with built-in beds in each room under which coal was often stored. The cottages were normally built on land fit for no other purpose and therefore likely to be damp clay. It was common to find that the floorboards had been laid on the earth, and sometimes stopped in line with the beds so that the occupants slept, if not over their coal supplies, over bare earth.

Pit villages, said one writer in the mid-nineteenth century, managed to combine the inconveniences of a country village in terms of facilities with the ugliness of the meaner parts of a manufacturing town. A typical one consisted of 'some half a dozen rows of perfectly uniform one-storied cottages, the intersecting lanes dotted with ash heaps and middens with, in rainy weather, perfect sloughs of mud formed round the hills of refuse. On the outskirts rise one or two modest-looking dissenting chapels, as unadorned as though the line of beauty typified the path to destruction, and about as big as ordinary-sized parlours. . . . All around stretches a labyrinth of deep rutted miry crossroads, through which, in wintry weather, the wayfarer wades rather than walks.' It was not until the ideas of the Garden City movement began to influence colliery companies just before the First World

War that the dreary chequerboard pattern was relinquished; Ashington, the largest pit village in the northeast of England, built in the 1890s and 1900s, was cast firmly in the old mould, though progress was represented by 'gardens dotted with outside privies'. It was a pity that colliery companies did not take up the sensible suggestions of a professor of the Newcastle School of Medicine, who in 1840 had criticized the unpaved and undrained spaces between the facing fronts of pit rows which presented 'along the centre one long ash heap and dunghill'. How much better, he suggested, to arrange the cottages in triangles so that ashes and rubbish might be concealed at their backs, with privies provided, while the fronts could face on to a green where children could play and washing might be dried. He noted also that pit pumping engines produced vast quantities of hot water which went to waste, but could be used for baths. But in the matter of planning he was sixty years ahead of his time, and, on the question of district heating, over a century.

Nevertheless, conditions in Northumberland and Durham, which inspired the professor's remarks, were well above the barbarity of the Scottish and Welsh pit villages. William Morrison, a doctor 'engaged in the Countess of Durham's collieries', reported in 1841 that the typical cottage had two rooms with a pantry and a low-roofed attic above. Most were well furnished and warm, he said, and 'in a well-ordered house, the final adjustment of affairs for the night presents a gratifying picture of social comfort'. He may well have felt it part of his duty to the Lambton family to put the best gloss he could on the facts, but sub-commissioner John Leifchild, who often showed himself to be not easily deceived by the sweet talk of owners, agents and others with official obligations, testified in the same year to the comfort of many of the colliers' homes, often, as he noted, furnished with eight-day clocks (a significant consumer durable of the time), good items of furniture and even, in two houses, mahogany four-poster beds, all paid for on instalments.

No doubt one reason for the superiority of housing in the northeast was the rapid expansion of the coal industry there once the steam engine made it possible to win coal at greater depths. Setting up a new colliery, with its attendant village, in a hitherto barren area, the owner was obliged to provide reasonable housing. He might be unfortunate enough to attract the sweepings from other coalfields, but if he was canny and offered enough amenities to attract the steady man, perhaps with some conditions written into the agreement as to sobriety and the keeping of pigs (in some parts of Scotland prohibition of pigs was a means of keeping out the Irish), he could equip himself with a law-abiding, industrious force who would repay him with loyalty and the service of his family. At Coxhoe in south Durham, for example, a new village was built in the 1830s to provide labour for the newly opened Clarence Hetton pit. It consisted of rows of blue-slated cottages, 'exceedingly neat, and as like to one another as so many soldiers are like to each other', with stone walls plastered with lime. Carts delivered house coal each day, and at the same time removed ashes and refuse. Houses for families consisted of a large front room, about fourteen or fifteen feet square, and a back room about two thirds as big, with an adjoining pantry. There was one large bedroom upstairs. This arrangement permitted the segregation of the sexes for sleeping, and the separation of parents from children, and also enabled members of the family to wash in private in the back room. For couples without children, there was a smaller version with only one downstairs room.

Unfortunately, even in the northeast, such model developments were not widely copied. A report of 1865 that pitmen's cottages in the northeast were the worst and dearest in the country, except for Monmouthshire, was certainly an exaggeration, but there certainly were some black spots. At Prudhoe, east of Newcastle, a hundred cottages had for their water supply 'one small dribbling stream, little thicker than a pencil', and it was said that at Mickley, a mile or two away, up to one hundred women could be seen queueing for water, and those who got up in the middle of the night to avoid the crowd 'even then find others waiting their turns at two or three o'clock'. There was not a single privy in the village, which had a population of 600, and the colliers did not want privies, suspecting the owners of wanting to make more money by selling the dung to farmers.

In the northwest, Wigan seemed to have the worst conditions. The typical arrangement was 'one up, one down', as many as six or seven people sleeping in one bed. Two or more families might share one of these hovels, which, because there was only one door, could not be adequately ventilated. In most houses, according to Mr Latham, the Chief Constable of Wigan, furniture was almost unheard of. Colliers did not feel the want of chairs, he said, as it was their habit to squat on the heels of their clogs. John Davis, collier of Wigan, had a chair and a rude bench; but that was all. He was discovered 'looking out of his window as dirty as it was possible for a man to be'. There was no food in the house. Nearby lived Michael Fairhurst with his five children, one of whom said she had not eaten for a day. A neighbour reported that she had given Fairhurst some bread and cheese one day, and 'he had eaten it like a tiger'. When the inspector gave the children some money for food, he was 'quite shocked with the look of ravenous joy with which they received it'. In this part of Wigan, the streets were unsewered and there were few privies, the few that there were being in such a state that the more respectable families refused to use them. Even in Lancashire, however, there were brighter spots. A benevolent coalmaster at Newton-le-Willows, for example, had provided a row of thirty four-roomed houses, each with a small garden, and detached privies and pigsties. The houses 'were, with a few exceptions, exceedingly neat and tidy, and several were remarkably nicely kept, and well stocked with furniture'.

The rapid expansion of the South Wales coalfield, resulting in the importation of a large immigrant workforce, caused special problems. The sloping sites on which most of the pit rows were built, with little or no attempt to drain off the flow of water from the mountains, did not help. Even newly built houses were without privies. The cottages at Hirwaun, near Merthyr Tydfil, were 'nothing more than mud cabins, in many instances a deserted cowshed converted into a human habitation; a rude thatch forms the roof, and apparently to avoid the storms that sweep along the plain, they are built in every hollow that can be found, where of course they receive the drainage of the surrounding elevations.' A more cheerless place could scarcely be found, reported an inspector in 1841. 'Even the school which I visited here more resembles a stable than a place for education,' he added. Such basic housing was also to be found in Scotland; near the Redding collieries of the Duke of Hamilton in Stirlingshire, there was an area called the Divities, a set of cottages built by squatting colliers. The walls were of turf (divots) and the roofs were thatched with reeds and heather. There was no drainage, and each cottage stood in its own morass.

But some observers could record steady improvements. Dr

Matthew Webb started in general practice in Wellington, Shropshire, in 1805. The colliers' houses then were 'a sort of barracks in long rows, with no upstairs apartments, but entirely on the ground floor, and very damp and dirty; their privies and piggeries too near to the dwellings and there was no proper drainage'. The succeeding years brought changes for the better, and by the 1830s the newer houses were reasonably well ventilated, with upstairs bedrooms, gardens, and their privies and piggeries set well away from the living quarters. Cabbages, potatoes and flowers grew in the gardens and allotments, and some men cultivated up to a quarter of an acre. It was due to these improvements, Dr Webb believed, that the area had largely escaped the cholera epidemic of 1832–33, which had badly affected the surrounding districts and had killed some 60,000 people in Britain.

It should not have been surprising – though the connection was not made until later in the nineteenth century – that the quality of life inside a house was related to conditions outside. The Coxhoe development referred to earlier was based on the premise that colliers' wives would stay at home 'to perform their domestic duties and to attend to the happiness of their own families'. In Northumberland and Durham, women had not been employed in the pits since the end of the eighteenth century, and probably not in any numbers for a couple of generations before that, so that they had had the opportunity to cultivate domestic skills; though it was often regretted that the lack of opportunities for girls to go into service, owing to the absence of a middle class in pit areas, deprived them of the chance to learn by example and so improve standards in the pit cottages once they married. Coxhoe could contradict this view. Inside one house, a collier was discovered 'clean-washed, sitting at the table and luxuriating over baked potatoes and broiled bacon, with a jug of beer, and seemed to feel very happy. The wife seemed happy in making him comfortable'. The house was clean and well furnished, with 'an eight-day clock, a chest of drawers, with brass handles and ornaments, reaching from the floor to the ceiling, a four-poster bed with a large coverlet composed of squares of printed calico tastefully arranged, and bright saucepans and other tinware utensils displayed on the walls'. At Coxhoe, this was not exceptional, though 'there are some women who are neither so attentive to themselves, their children or their houses as their husbands have a right to expect'. The houses had no gardens, but there were allotments for those who wanted to grow potatoes or even flowers. It was said that in some villages thereabouts colliers often 'carried off the palm from the gentlemen's gardeners' at local flower shows, which must certainly have caused some grumbling in the gardens of the big houses. But Coxhoe was a remarkable village for its time, in many ways. The cottages were rent-free, and so was as much coal as a family could use, though cartage had to be paid for. The colliers were at an advantage, too, in living close to their work, leaving them more time and effort to attend to things at home.

In fact, pit wives were no more likely than other women to be slatternly, and many of them performed remarkable feats of housekeeping. Sarah Wood, whose husband was working at Brown Top pit near Halifax in 1841, gave an account of her budget. She had nine children, two of whom were hurriers and two hewers. All lived at home and, with her husband, brought in between thirty and forty shillings a week. They lived chiefly on oatmeal and milk, wheatcake, a pound and a half or two pounds of mutton a week, bacon and potatoes, and sometimes a drop of home-brew. It sounds like a struggle, but not impossible. But the odds could be heavily against a pitman's wife. Phoebe Gilbert, of Watnall near Nottingham, had four sons by two marriages. One died in a shaft accident, another in an explosion. Her first husband died at fifty-seven from chronic asthma. She did her best with her surviving children, both teenagers and working in the pit; she had seen to it that they could read, knew some of the Bible, did not swear, get drunk or misbehave. At Ringley Bridge in Lancashire Peggy Lowe overcame the economic blast of widowhood by taking a job at Foster's pit as an onsetter, hooking loaded corves on to the rope at the bottom of the shaft. 'Her house' it was reported, 'is quite exemplary in the way of cleanliness,' and even at work she was neat and tidy, with a low-crowned hat and a close-fitting cap to keep the coal dust out of her hair.

Apart from the steady improvement in housing, the other important influence on the standard of living towards the end of the eighteenth century and at the beginning of the nineteenth, at least in some areas, was the Nonconformist movement and, in particular, Methodism. It was, indeed, among the colliers of Kingswood, to the east of Bristol, that the foundations of Methodism were laid in 1739. The Kingswood men had a particularly fierce reputation. They 'feared not God and regarded not men', it was said, and the year before George Whitefield started his series of open-air conversion meetings among them sixty Kingswood colliers had been arrested after a street riot in which public houses were vandalized and passers-by robbed. But he attracted crowds of up to 20,000 to his preaching, and was gratified, he wrote later, to see 'the white gutters made by their tears, which plentifully fell down their black cheeks'. Whitefield's friend John Wesley, who had previously opposed open-air meetings, attended one of the gatherings and became converted to 'field-preaching', which thereafter became the principal tool of Methodist evangelism. And it was from Bristol that Wesley set out on the career of itinerant preaching that was to occupy the remaining fifty-two years of his life.

However, despite the reputation of the achievements at Kingswood in the annals of Methodism, they should not be overstated. There was no overnight conversion, for all the colliers' repentant tears. For many years the people of Bristol and, on occasions, Bath, Gloucester and even Hereford, continued to retreat, as they had become accustomed to do, behind barred doors and shuttered windows when it was known that the Kingswood colliers were coming to town; and in 1753 the Kingswood men, protesting at the high price of corn, marched into Bristol 2000 strong with a petition, broke the windows of the Council House and, when they eventually retreated, took hostages. An account of the area in about 1800 – after sixty years of preaching – spoke of the colliers as 'the terror of the surrounding neighbourhoods, and for gross ignorance, rudeness and irreligion, almost without parallels in any Christian community. . . . You could not ride through some of the villages and hamlets without being insulted by the boys, who would throw stones at both horse and rider, without provocation. "The Kingswood colliers" was then a phrase that conveyed every idea offensive to civilization, order and religion.' But by 1840, it could be reported that there was 'as much decorum in the manners of the population as is witnessed in the generality of rural districts', which, although it sounds like a qualified tribute, was certainly an improvement on the general misrule of earlier years; though neglect of public worship, it was noted, was still prevalent among the younger colliers.

At first, colliers were no more inclined than anyone else to accept

Wesley's preaching, and in various parts of the country participated with a will in the disturbances and threats against him organized, in many instances, by magistrates and the Anglican clergy. One of the worst outbreaks of violence was at Wednesbury in 1743, when a mob of colliers attacked the homes of known Methodists and destroyed all their furniture. According to Wilson Jones's *History of the Black Country*, there was a popular parody in those parts of the evangelistic hymn 'I heard the voice of Jesus say/Come unto me and rest' which ran in part:

> I heard the voice of Twiggins say,
> Come let us work no more.
> Lay down thy 'ammer and thy tongs
> And beg from door to door.
>
> John Wesley had a bonny 'oss
> As lean as ever was sin.
> We took him down to Hayseech Brook
> And shoved him headfirst in.

But although Wesley suffered many indignities during his ministry, there is no evidence that being shoved headfirst into Hayseech Brook was one of them.

In other areas, Wesley met with a better reception – notably in Newcastle-upon-Tyne, the scene of his first preaching in the North and subsequently the focal point of Methodism there. 'I walked down to Sandgate,' he wrote in his journal after his 1742 visit, 'the poorest and most contemptible part of the town; and, standing at the end of the street with John Taylor [his servant], began to sing the Hundredth Psalm. Three or four people came out to see what was the matter, who soon increased to four or five hundred. I suppose there might be twelve or fifteen hundred, before I had done preaching.' He spoke again in the evening of the same day and was begged to stay on; but he had business elsewhere. It was the first of many visits, and it was said that colliers would come into Newcastle and sleep in the open to hear him preach the following morning. Occasionally, some colliers may have found Wesley's message obscure; commenting in his journal on a pit accident that happened while he was visiting Whitehaven in Cumberland in 1759 in which a man was killed and three horribly burned, he noted that 'life or death was welcome, for God had restored the light of His countenance'.

It was after Wesley's death in 1791 that Methodism really began to capture the popular imagination, helped a great deal by the split in the movement in 1808 which created the Primitive Methodist Church. The Wesley message was too severe, and his services too reminiscent of the Church of England, for many tastes. A meeting of the 'Prims' could be relied upon to be more exciting, as this account of a Primitive Methodist crusade in County Durham in the 1830s shows: 'Fallings were common, as many as fourteen being seen on the floor at once. At a love feast at Bishop Auckland the people fell in all directions, and there was a strange mingling of shouts, groans and hallelujahs. . . . Confirmed gamblers burnt their dice, cards and books of enchantment; drunkards, hopeless incurable sots, were freed from the dread tyranny of fiery appetite; pugilists, practiced and professional, and cock-fighters of terrible experience turned from their brutalities.' The singing of Charles Wesley's decorous and melodious hymns, as practised by the Wesleyans, could hardly compete with this, and it was not surprising that the popular name for the Primitive Methodists – which they used themselves with evident pride – was 'the Ranters', not to be confused with the pantheistic sect of Commonwealth times. Observing their success, other denominations such as the Congregationalists and the Baptists and the New Connexion (yet another Methodist breakaway group) moved in on the coalfields, giving a delicious choice for colliers of a religious frame of mind and a refuge for those who, for one reason or another, fell out with a particular chapel. By 1852 the Ranters, with over 100,000 members and many times that number attending their services and Sunday schools, were neck and neck with the Wesleyans. The Baptists, much dislocated by schism, were some way behind, though they too could provide their excitements: at the pit village of Llancyach in Glamorgan in 1841, there was a mass baptism, by total immersion, of course, in a local stream. The occasion, according to the village innkeeper, 'was nearly attended by fatal consequences as a number of the curious who went to witness the ceremony fell into the water and several were seriously injured, and some nearly drowned'.

It cannot have been easy to persuade people who had worked underground for twelve hours a day, five or six days in the week, and at the hardest work under heaven, to give up the seventh to chapel and Sunday school, but the explosion of Nonconformism in pit areas in the first half of the nineteenth century was a phenomenon that has rarely been equalled in Britian's political or religious history. It bears comparison, perhaps, with another great upsurge of popular feeling, though shorter-lived, which is equally incomprehensible to modern eyes: the war fever of 1914. In some places, religious fervour spread below ground, unbelievable though it is that those who worked in the pits at that time could have been receptive to news of a worse place, called hell. By the 1830s, there were pits in Staffordshire where prayer meetings were held each day after the midday break, and the men would not work with anyone who did not take part. The master of one pit allowed an extra five minutes for the prayers. There were also occasional visits to the workings by preachers, with surface workers descending to hear them, which, according to one report, 'has been the cause of turning many a poor sinner to God, and to amendment of their lives'. Perhaps some of the converts tended to be 'pi'; it was said that in some pits they split to the master if they heard a workmate swear, and the man would lose a day's beer allowance. Though Methodists preached against strong drink, the Nonconformist movement was as yet not formally linked to teetotalism, and indeed the Wesleyans distanced themselves (perhaps because many prominent Wesleyans were brewers) from the Band of Hope movement until well into the 1870s. In any case, beer was reckoned in many areas to be essential to the work and good health of the miner, and in Staffordshire was provided by the butties for men and boys alike. 'We call the teetotallers water-bellies,' said a 15-year-old Staffordshire hurrier. 'A miner could not do without drinking beer. It is good for the constitution.' (His turn of phrase is surprising, but he seems to have been a boy of parts. He had read *Pilgrim's Progress*, Bunyan's *Holy War*, the Bible, the Prayer Book, and some books of sermons. He prayed twice a day, went to school twice on Sundays, and helped in his father's cabbage and potato garden.) In Warwickshire, colliers were said to 'love gospel sermons' such as the Ranters preached. The large Methodist chapel at Coalpit Bank, Coalbrookdale in Shropshire, attracted between 500 and 700 children to its school twice each Sunday. Not that the influence of Sunday schools was always impressive, however. Daniel Edwards, sixteen, who worked at the Gilvach Vargoed Colliery in Glamorgan, was a regular attender at the Wesleyan Sunday school, but he didn't know what for and didn't know how many commandments there were. At that time Sunday schools did not restrict themselves to religious instruction but also taught the 'three Rs'. In this they were not particularly successful, as their untrained teachers – often injured colliers who had been found a light job – relied heavily on the parrot-learning method. Day schools were not necessarily much better. At Coleford in Gloucestershire, a public-spirited group tried to establish an infant school for collier children, but made an ill-judged choice of master and it failed. 'This man, being rather pragmatical, and an accomplished cockney, used to question the children after this manner: "*Vich* is this substance? *Hanimal, wegitable* or mineral?*"* it was reported; and would respond when they failed to understand his language, "*Vy, wegitable,* to be sure." The young rogues used to laugh at him; and, of course, all respect and subordination were at an end.' It was perhaps understandable that standards of learning in such schools were low. One Lancashire boy, who had been to day school, reported that he had heard of the Queen but did not know who *he* was. A Halifax boy of thirteen at first thought there were six days in the week, but afterwards remembered that there was another day, on which father got tipsy.

Even where a day school had been established this was no guarantee that it would be taken advantage of. There was the sad case of Squire Butterfield, master of the Netherthorp Free School near Staveley in Derbyshire. The school was established in the late eighteenth century, and was rebuilt and enlarged in 1804. It was open to all the sons of the parishioners of Staveley for classical instruction, but the master could charge for lessons in reading, writing and arithmetic. Perhaps this odd order of priorities led to its downfall. At one time there were forty pupils, but by 1840 Squire Butterfield had none left. He could not remember how many years it was since he had a scholar, but it was a long time, he said. 'They dropped off one after another, without assigning any reason.' He scarcely missed a day without going into the school, but it was years since he found anyone there. However, he was still taking a salary of about twenty-five pounds a year.

In the northeast, pit villages were often in areas remote from established parishes, which gave the Nonconformist chapels an advantage over the Church of England, especially as they made use of voluntary lay preachers, who were often themselves miners. 'Much praise,' said one report from south Durham, 'is everywhere bestowed on the Wesleyan and Primitive Methodists for their zealous and successful exertions in instructing and civilizing the destitute colliers.' But not everyone bestowed praise. As early as 1739 the *Gentleman's Magazine*, commenting on Whitefield's preaching at Kingswood, voiced one common apprehension: 'The industry of the inferior people in a society is the great source of its prosperity. But if one man, like the Reverend Mr Whitefield, should have it in his power, by his preaching, to detain five or six thousands of the vulgar from their daily labour, what a loss, in a little time, may this bring to the public! For my part, I shall expect to hear of a prodigious rise in the price of coals about the city of Bristol if this gentleman proceeds, as he has begun, with his charitable lectures to the colliers of Kingswood.' But it was the danger of sedition that inspired much anti-Methodist agitation. As late as 1812 there was an attempt to bring in a bill to ban all Methodist meetings. The Combination Acts, prohibiting meetings for trade-union purposes, were still in force; if Methodists were allowed to gather together, supposedly to read the Bible and pray, who knew what else might not be on their agenda? This fear was revived in 1834, when it was discovered that the six Tolpuddle Martyrs, who were transported for administering illegal oaths at a trade-union meeting, were all Wesleyans, and three of them local preachers. The prejudice persisted in the 1840s among many owners and colliery managers in the northeast. George Johnson, manager of three Tyneside collieries, noted that when there was a dispute between master and men 'these educated persons, or Methodists, are most decidedly the hardest to deal with. This is not always from taking the correct view of the nature of the disputes, but from self-sufficiency and self-satisfaction with their superiority.' It was the self-education of the Methodists that Mr Johnson objected to most. He disapproved 'of that overeducation which might unfit a man for labour in the pits, by rendering him discontented', though he would not object to more instruction about methods of colliery working. The Countess of Durham's agent at Biddick, near Lambton, added that 'a class of self-sufficient leaders, who are generally local preachers, and who are most decidedly the most difficult to control . . . urge on the others to acts of great insubordination'. There were worries in some quarters, too, of the effect on the morals of the colliers and their families of the 'stirring, exciting character' of Methodism, while a coalowner at Earsdon, near Whitley Bay, Thomas Taylor, was concerned with the Methodists' defects of character. They were, he said, 'fond of becoming preachers, class leaders etc., themselves, and this opens the door to a vast deal of vanity and conceit; in so much that I suspect there is more of vainglory and hypocrisy than of any sounder feeling.' In pointing to the democratic and self-governing traditions of Methodism, Mr Taylor may well have been unconsciously peeping into the boiling cauldron of the future history of the Labour movement. It was true enough that the experience of running meetings and fulfilling the offices of Methodist chapels gave many men a taste for affairs and an ability to manage them which they later exercised in the trade unions and the Labour Party; and in the Durham coalfield in particular the later nineteenth-century histories of Primitive Methodism and the colliers' unions ran hand in hand. There were, for example, John Bell, who spent sixty-seven years in the pits and almost as many as a Methodist class leader and local preacher, and who was elected secretary of his miners' lodge, only to be dismissed from the pit; and Peter Lee, after whom the Durham new town was named, who went down the pit at ten and returned after a period of emigration to become a local miners' leader and county councillor, and who was a lifelong Primitive Methodist and spent almost every Sunday of his adult life in the pulpit. Durham seems to have been outstanding in linking the Ranters and the unions so closely, but other areas could quote similar examples – including, of course, South Wales. Nye Bevan, who went into the pit at fourteen, came from a Methodist background. And in Scotland, Keir Hardie – who like Tom Mann went into the pit at ten, six years after the minimum age had been raised to twelve – although an atheist, learned his public-speaking skills in the associated Temperance movement. Small wonder that a former Labour Party secretary, Morgan Phillips, used to say that the father of English Socialism was not Karl Marx, but John Wesley.

The successes of Nonconformism caught the Anglican church short, and it took the best part of the nineteenth century to catch up – by which time it was too late. At South Church in Durham, where there was in fact no church, it was said that for this reason the layabouts of Bishop Auckland to the north and Shilton to the south – in both of which towns 'good order' was kept of a Sunday by the clergy – flocked to the village, 'and in the adjacent lanes on Sunday afternoons may be seen groups of characters gambling and otherwise improperly employing themselves'. Such unseemly goings-on were partly checked after the creation of the county police forces in 1839, for although an isolated village constable could be no match for a gang of Shilton lads he could perform such useful offices as rigidly enforcing Sunday drinking laws so that the beer houses opened only after one o'clock, well clear of morning service. According to some evidence fighting decreased and Sabbath observance gained after the appointment of the police, but as most of the evidence came from coalowners it may not be reliable. The increasing attention being given to conditions in mining areas after Lord Shaftesbury began to take an interest in them was an embarrassment to many owners, who were also magistrates and had control of the police, and who did not want their own pit villages to be shown up as scenes of wild or irregular behaviour. Nevertheless, there were owners who exercised their consciences so long as this did not interfere too drastically with their profits, and there were villages where religious observance was positively fervent. In the new village of South Hetton near Durham, built in 1831 for the opening of a new pit, the Anglican church, erected largely at the expense of the owners, had congregations of between eighty and one hundred each Sunday, the Wesleyan chapel even more, and there was also a Ranters' chapel. Each place also ran a Sunday school. A 14-year-old South Hetton driver testified to the effectiveness of living in such a well-disciplined community. After fifteen hours in the pit, he spent two hours each evening at school: 'I hurt myself very sore to get scholarship,' he said. He attended the Ranters' chapel and was a member of the Temperance Society, having 'signed his hand' when he was eleven. After chapel on Sunday morning, his father, who was not always able to attend, examined him on the sermon. There were another two hours' chapel in the afternoon. The boy was then free to read the Bible, a *History of England* or teetotal books.

The charm of the chapels must have been, for many of their members, the fact that they were a part of their lives where they could direct their own affairs, away from human interference at least. But some masters were not beyond harnessing the appeal of religion in the cause of Mammon, at the same time defusing its potential as a source of rebellion. Such were the Stansfield and

Briggs families, who ran pits in partnership at Flockton, between Huddersfield and Barnsley, and whose wives and families had interested themselves in education. The Sunday regime for the village children was fairly punishing. School began at nine with prayers, continued with hymns and readings, and was followed at 10.20, after a glass of water, by a half-mile walk in crocodile to the Anglican church. The walk at least must have been a relief after an hour of standing 'still and straight' with your hands behind your back. Afternoon school began at 1.45 and there were more hymns and instructions in the creed and catechism, followed by another walk to church at three. To encourage attendance, the children were bribed with penny tickets, of which they could earn four for a full Sunday stint, and with which they could buy books. The owners' wives and families took part in the religious instruction and in a number of other community activities, including a Temperance Society run on lines both voluntary and Draconian, a peculiar combination. Signing the pledge was voluntary, but once signed it was binding and backsliders faced instant dismissal from the pit. The Flockton system sounds pretty unctuous, and it is not surprising that many children said that they were too tired on Sunday to spend it in chapel. It is worth noting, too, that the existence of Sunday schools freed pit proprietors from any duty they might have felt to establish or support day schools, which apart from the expense might have interfered with child labour. The Spartan tradition persisted at Flockton, however. In the middle 1860s there was a challenging list of Sunday school rules, which were read out from time to time. It was forbidden to bring sweets, and girls must not enter school in pattens. Punishments included a wooden clapper – in favour of which it was said that its bark was worse than its bite – and lesser offenders were required to stand on a form holding aloft the chapel Bible.

The Briggs and Stansfield families had no difficulty in reconciling their Sunday piety with proprietorship of a pit where, on Henry Briggs's own admission, the children of large families went down as early as six years old and there was a boy of seven hurrying, on his own, a loaded corf weighing four hundredweight. (It was hurry or nothing for children at Flockton; no trappers were employed, supposedly on grounds of safety, but more probably for economy's sake, since while it was for getters to pay their own hurriers the payment of trappers was the management's responsibility.) Covering about five and a half miles a shift, hurriers at Flockton heaved thirty corves a day. Mr Briggs objected on principle (like most coalmasters) to government interference in the operation of the pits. No wonder. Government inspectors might have discovered that, for example, although he declared the working day at Flockton to be from six in the morning to five in the evening at most, the children often started at four.

In Scotland the colliers were denied, in most pits, any regard for their human condition, but at least they were also spared the attentions of hollow piety. In many parts the expansion of towns and villages had been so rapid after the arrival in 1719 of Scotland's first Newcomen engine that religion had no chance to catch up. Nonconformist religious ideas failed notably to penetrate north of the border, and, of course, the spirit of the Church of Scotland was not sympathetic to evangelism, at any rate at home. Meanwhile, the native Roman Catholic Church of the Irish who flocked to the pits of the west of Scotland laboured until almost the middle of the nineteenth century under great difficulty and prejudice. With a few notable exceptions, there was too much greed in the Scottish pits to admit much humanitarian or religious light; enlightenment cost money. But one of the exceptions was the Govan Colliery, near Glasgow, which had a number of educational and recreational facilities which it shared with its associated ironworks, including a twenty-five-piece works band (surely, in 1840, one of the first of its kind) and an eight-piece orchestra, the bandmaster being paid by the company. There was a liberal tradition at Govan which was developed and extended from 1822, when James Allan became colliery manager. Early in the century, Govan was one of the first (and remained one of the few) Scottish managements to fund a school, but what happened to it illustrates how abjectly the Church of Scotland failed in its pastoral duties. Having established the school, the Govan owners trusted its management to the local minister. He appointed a succession of young, temporary, inexperienced and quite unsuitable masters and made no attempt to inspect or control the place, thus ignoring the requirements of his office that he should visit his entire parish each year and report on its moral, physical and temporal condition. The masters' behaviour upset the parents – the reticence of the reports on the masters' offences suggests that some of these, at least, were sexual – and the children were gradually withdrawn, reducing the school by 1826 to the point of closure. James Allan then vested its management in a committee of workmen, a startling innovation for that time and one that would not have met with the approval of those coalmasters of northeast England who feared for the results of giving their men experience of self-government. All parents of children between six and twelve were obliged to make monthly payments for the school, and it prospered under its new management though not all parents who paid let their children take advantage of it. This was the first of a series of remarkable initiatives undertaken by Mr Allan. It was followed by a workmen's committee to deal with disputes and wages, a 'Friendly and Free Labour Society' to support the sick and injured ('and to protect the workmen from the threats and intimidations of the combined'; though in the event it was never required to do so, doubtless as a result of Mr Allan's enlightened management) and a funeral fund. A library was established, with 1400 volumes which were exchanged at the rate of one hundred a week, and in 1841 there were fortnightly lectures on moral and scientific subjects, with magic-lantern illustrations. It was an enterprise in the spirit of Robert Owen's New Lanark, not far away, and was no doubt influenced by it. Moreover, it was not loaded with religion, and the various conditions by which contributions were paid for the friendly society and its associated funds were laid down not by the masters but by the workforce; a refreshing contrast to Flockton.

Govan in the 1840s, with its peaceable colliers and ironworkers watching moral and scientific lantern slides, queueing up to change their library books and running their own school, presents a contrast to nearby Airdrie, which was anything but peaceful. 'There is not a worse place out of hell,' one of the partners in the Gartsherrie Collieries said in 1841. Murders could be committed every day and not be heard of. The police had evacuated the area, and Sunday drinking laws were widely flouted, but the authorities were afraid to interfere. Some men spent two thirds of their wages on drink. Men who had tried to cultivate their gardens had given up because their vegetables were stolen. The Roman Catholic priest in Airdrie, the Reverend Daniel Callaghan, attributed much of the trouble to the Irish, who sometimes lodged as many as fourteen to one small room. Over to the east in Midlothian, Inveresk was another black spot, according to Dr William Stevenson, in practice there. He found the colliers 'a dissipated, drunken, improvident and dirty set of people, with little or no notion of anything but drunkenness and rioting'. Some worked only three or four days a week and drank the rest of the time away, between bouts of thrashing their wives and children. They bought whisky by the gallon, which cost about two days' pay for a hewer. Licensing was virtually uncontrolled.

For all that has been said about the significance of the chapels, and they *were* significant in many ways, not least in their influence on behaviour, this was political rather than numerical. Victorian Britain was not such a God-fearing society as is often supposed by those with a rosy view of Victorian values, and there is a precise piece of evidence on this. Once and once only, in 1851, the census included a question on whether people had or had not attended a place of worship the previous Sunday, and the answer was that over half had attended neither church nor chapel. (Perhaps even more worrying for the Establishment was the fact that almost as many had gone to a chapel or Roman Catholic service as had favoured the Church of England.) An equally instructive question would have been to ask whether people had or had not, on the previous weekend, visited a place of public drinking. Despite the advances of Nonconformism, despite all the friendly societies and magic-lantern lectures and gardening clubs, despite the musical evenings at Flockton, as a result of which 'collier boys can be heard singing and whistling the beautiful airs from Handel, Haydn, Mozart and Spohr', the main leisure pursuit of the working class, and in particular of colliers, was drinking. It was suggested in some quarters that the educators and the temperance enthusiasts might have had more success if they had set their sights lower, not conducting their efforts 'with too strict a hand, or under the imposing titles of Athenaeum, Mechanics' Institute, or Temperance Hall, but rather in an inviting and conciliatory spirit than in the exclusive tone which too often mars the effect of such well-intended attempts'. This was, of course, the policy to be adopted many years later by the Salvation Army. Meanwhile, drinking was given a great boost, to the joy of the brewers, in 1830 when, in what turned out to be an ill-judged attempt to curb the sales of gin, beer was freed from tax and any householder was allowed to open his door for its sale, free of licence or control. The result was the creation of 31,000 new beer outlets, while gin consumption was only slightly and temporarily checked and whisky drinking continued to increase. It was 1869 before this unfortunate piece of legislation was withdrawn, but by then a huge new market for liquor had been created which was not brought under control until the severe curtailment of the licensing laws in the First World War.

It was the view of the Reverend Henry Berkin, Rector of Holy Trinity Church in the Forest of Dean, that the Beer Act had incalculably injured the morals of the neighbourhood. He had seen, since it came into operation, boys of twelve *staggering drunk*. The new pot houses induced colliers to spend their money away from their families and destroyed their domestic habits. John Trotter Thomas, who owned several coalworks in the Forest, agreed. The beer shops were, he said, little better than brothels. As a Baptist, he had seen 'melancholy instances of religious men falling victims of sotting in consequence of visiting these houses'. They had made drinking acceptable to people who would never have gone to a public house of the old style. He would prefer to see beer retailed for consumption at home, so as to remove the temptation of 'companionship in drinking, to the selfish expenditure of wages in liquor, leaving wives and children in destitution and want'. Students of attitudes to drinking will notice an interesting contrast with a contemporary obsession, the easy availability of alcohol through supermarkets, which has certainly made drinking acceptable to people who would never had gone to a public house – so it is said – but yet transfers heavy drinking to the home.

The Temperance Societies might try their best with, as one who attended their meetings recalled, 'diagrams of human organs before and after maltreatment by alcohol', and even semi-animated magic-lantern slides on a similar theme, but the demon drink was, it seemed, invincible. If drink couldn't be bought, it could be made, and an ingenious group of Newcastle colliers hit upon a brilliant wheeze in 1822 when they set up an illicit still in the old workings of a pit, fuelling it from coal still remaining in the seam and dispersing the smoke through the abandoned galleries.

It would be tedious to recite the evidence of the monumental drinking capacity of the British miner, but most observers agree that although the Temperance movement had some small, local successes, drinking continued undiminished until price and the licensing laws together checked it. It was, of course, a pastime not

Top: The nightly ritual in front of the kitchen range before the days of pit baths. It was not until 1947 and nationalization that most miners could clean up before going home
Left: Two colliers in the family
Right: A Nottinghamshire miner comes home

Above: 'Little Tick', the pit pony. The names of pit ponies and horses were traditional

Left: Setting a prop in a Nottinghamshire pit

Below: Snap time. In many pits snap was at the mercy of rats and a boy would be set to guard the tins

Ramming a powder charge

A deputy examines a roadway at the beginning of the shift. In the better-regulated pits, only when he had completed his inspection and reported that all was well would the men start work

A putter at Tinsley Park Colliery, near Sheffield

Undercutting and filling

Inspecting a roof fall

Hewing in the Douglas Bank pit near Wigan

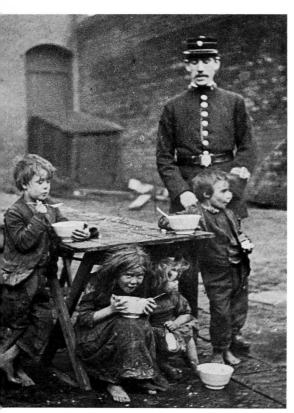

Above left: The Public Hall at Aberaman, originally a miners' institute

Above right: Hauling with a pony in the Rhondda, *c.* 1900

Below: Great Western Colliery Band, 1902 South Wales and Monmouthshire champions

Above: Underground work for women was outlawed by the Victorians, although they laboured on at the pit bank, together with disabled men, into this century. Here, *c*. 1900, pit-bank girls line up for their pay and are harangued by a pit official. They seem to be standing to attention

Below: The morning after the Senghenydd disaster. Note that every house has its blinds drawn and also, in the foreground, the examples of the basest kind of miners' housing in South Wales

Women coal bearers in a
Scottish pit, 1850s

In the 'thick coal' of south Staffordshire, 1850s

Putting, 1850s

Undercutting, 1850s

Undercutting at Frog Lane pit. Note the getter's tally number chalked above the face

Pit girls tipping at a Wigan pit

confined to colliers. Henry Worsley, writing in 1849, cast its shadow far wider. Drink, he said, was 'the cause of causes . . . the arcanum which is at the bottom of the whole superstructure of our national depravity', which was perhaps coming on a bit strong. However, it was certainly true that the weekend was, in collier districts as in many others, no time for an innocent to be abroad.

The widespread practice of paying colliers fortnightly (the fortnight was reckoned to be 'the grand division of time to a miner'), though in some cases monthly, made most villages a Mecca every second Friday or Saturday, according to local custom, for tallymen, hucksters, quacks and chapmen of every degree. The charmers would be there, offering cures for everything from warts to pregnancy. (The development of the local press later did away with the necessity for the charmers to turn up in person; in the 1930s, colliers' wives and girlfriends who read the *Wrexham Advertiser* were invited to write to an address in south London for a sample packet of 'Pills for all ailments; never fail; special 1s.3d; free advice.') On pay night, chemists stayed open late, having knocked up fresh supplies of Godfrey's Cordial and similar opiates, so that childish cries should not disturb serious drinkers. The rates of interest extorted by tallymen were injurious, but they didn't sound too damaging to customers with a bit of drink inside them.

In most places, again subject to local custom, Saturday was the big night, closely rivalled by Sunday. Many were so devastated that they needed Monday to recover, and 'Collier Monday' or 'Saint Monday' was a widely recognized institution. Wages were often paid out at the public house, so that some of the money was exchanged very quickly indeed; many a clergyman and temperance enthusiast protested against this tradition, but the fact was that in few communities was there any other place suitable for the purpose. John Lawrence, a collier at Nuneaton, reported that 'after the reckoning the men go and refresh themselves, and carry home the remainder to their wives. Some hide a little money in their shoes, and when their wives go to settle with the baker or the butcher the men step back and have a little more.' The wives of the northeast of England, if one report is to be believed, were less fortunate. Gambling was rife in the pubs, although 'all this sort of thing is carefully concealed from the brewers, and it is only discovered when the wife complains of the small portion of his earnings brought home by her husband'. An additional toll in some areas, as will be seen later, was exacted by the truck system, 'tommy', which persisted in some areas long after Westminster had declared it beyond the law.

In the eighteenth century, an event would often be organized for Sunday: bull-baiting, or a dog-fight, or a main of cocks. The collier's coat of arms, it was said in Lancashire, was 'a stark naked child and a gamecock on a dunghill'. Bull- and bear-baiting became illegal in 1835, and cocking in 1849, but the effect of pressure to abandon these pastimes was to leave colliers with nothing to do of a Sunday but drink, while youngsters could only wander about and get up to mischief. By the early years of the nineteenth century the highly organized dog-fights of former years, with substantial amounts of money laid on the backs, or rather the jaws, of the protagonists, were dying out, but more casual dog-fighting in the street or the fields, arranged as it were between friends, continued; and indeed remained legal until 1911 unless prohibited by local bylaws.

The heartland of dog-fighting in Victorian times was the Black Country, where the Staffordshire bull terrier fought to clearly drawn rules which, it must be said, rendered the sport almost civilized, at least compared with the ruthless fight-to-the-death practices of earlier times and other places. Cock-fighting was, by 1849, already a declining sport, though of course it has never quite disappeared. Although modern sensibilities are properly offended at the thought of two goaded, steel-shod bantams set to tear each other to pieces (but not, curiously, by the less-even contest between fox and hounds), the care and training of a gamecock was an absorbing and demanding business which, if it had had any other end in view, would have been praised as a worthwhile and improving pastime. The birds were kept for two or three years before they were ready for the cockpit, meticulously fed and trained, and given as much attention as the objects of any modern fancy; and indeed the modern sublimation of cocking is the bantam fancy, in which competitive impulses are assuaged in the show ring rather than the cockpit. Cocking produced its characters as well as its champions, and it is hard to avoid regret at the passing of such as Ruff Moey (otherwise Ralph Moody, or Moses Whitehouse, or Moses Maggs, or perhaps he was a composite of all four), said to have been born round about 1780 in Wednesbury. Ruff, or Ralph, or Moses worked in the pit until an accident took off a leg and blinded him in one eye. Then he took to innkeeping, where he was well placed to develop his interest in cocking and dog-fighting. He is said to have intervened in a dog-fight in which both participants had been doped, and forced the bookmaker to repay all the stakes. Another of his claims to fame was that he was the last man to sell his wife in Wednesbury market, a transaction which, since 'neither in feature nor in figure was he prepossessing', may not have been too much regretted by Mrs Moey, Moody, Whitehouse or Maggs.

In the mid-nineteenth century, well before the Queensbury Rules were drawn up in 1866, prizefighting was still a popular sport, especially at holiday times. At Christmas 1840, there was a programme of twelve fights arranged at Rochdale. Lancashire style was 'up and down fighting', both men naked except for their clogs, and the fight ended with the winner choking his adversary until he gave way, whereupon the loser would be kicked in the head and about the body. It was reckoned good sport in that area, for extra entertainment, to get women drunk at the pub and then set them to fight, tearing each others' clothes until they were nearly naked. In the Wakefield area, more or less organized fights between women were common until recent years.

By the time of Queen Victoria's accession, occasions for entertainment were beginning to be more formalized and commercial, and once again it proved difficult for colliers to please their betters. Whereas in the great days of cocking and duck-hunting it was said that 'the things which they know in common with brute beasts are the only things they desire and pursue', middle-class observers now complained increasingly that pit folk were being corrupted by fairs, dances and theatres. Youth in particular was being seduced by 'spectacles, songs, etc., of an indecent nature', while one-act plays about Jack Sheppard, Dick Turpin, et al painted too tempting a picture of the life of crime. (Since the finale of such plays was usually a gallows scene, this argument is rather hard to follow.) Perhaps the critics themselves were too easily deceived by the large print on the playbills. *Love's Entertainments*, for example, which did a nationwide tour in 1851, and whose poster included such legends as 'Love in all Shapes' in extremely heavy type, turned out to be a demonstration of ventriloquism or, as Mr Love preferred to call it, 'the polyphonic art'. Still, it was perhaps marginally more interesting (though hardly seductive) and certainly more expensive than the magic-lantern show offered in the National Schoolroom at Wingate Grange Colliery in Durham – admission, fourpence for adults, one penny for under-twelves – when 'various SPLENDID VIEWS of CELEBRATED ARTISTES will be produced by a GENTLEMAN in a GRAND AND ATTRACTIVE PHANTASMAGORICAL EXHIBITION'. No amount of heavy type could conceal that this was going to be a pretty frosty evening. The prospect of pleasure was brighter at Workington in Cumberland, where a dancing master came regularly to the Cookson Colliery, though critics complained that the young people were 'far keener after the dancing lessons than the reading lessons'.

But for most pit folk, bound fast below from Monday to Friday or longer, high days and holidays were rare treats. In Warwickshire, the red-letter day was the day of the (literal) beanfeast, given by the landlord of the pub where the benefit club held its meetings: 'It is held at the time when the beans are just ripened. He prepares about two pecks full, and about twenty or thirty pounds of fat bacon and plenty of loaves of fresh bread. Every man takes his great bladed knife and cuts off a piece of bread and a slice of bacon, and helps himself to beans, and there is nothing left. Such a substantial meal requires to be washed down, and the men pay for their ale, so that the landlord is no loser by the hospitality of the festival.' This sounds more enjoyable than the ritualized version of the annual feast imposed by the Briggs and Stansfield families at Flockton, where, on the first Sunday in August, an examination of the Sundayschool scholars took place: 'The children assemble in the garden, where seats are prepared; after singing a hymn, and partaking of cake and milk, they are taken into the schoolroom, and there examined in the lessons of the preceding year. This Sunday is to the children one of the happiest of the year, and is anticipated by all parties with great pleasure,' according to Mrs Stansfield in 1841. But someone who took part in this joyless event in the mid-1860s remembered it as 'a toil of a pleasure, at all events to the younger portions. They were paraded in the neighbourhood until, at the finish, they were quite wearied'.

It was a common complaint about colliers that they took no thought for the morrow. If they did not drink their wages away, or spend them on worthless or indecent entertainments, then they indulged in good food – colliers were the first to eat the new season's duck and green peas, it was reported with disapproval from Warwickshire – or luxurious fitments, such as beds, for their houses. It was hard for a collier to do the right thing in his master's eyes. George Kenrick, a coalmaster in Monmouthshire, complained that, unlike farm workers, domestic servants and factory apprentices, who all earned less, colliers did not put their money in the savings bank, with the result that if they fell on hard times they had nothing to fall back on except parish relief. But perhaps the men were right not to put their trust in savings banks; there was considerable distress in the Rhondda in 1840 when a local savings bank collapsed with debts of nearly £2000. The various benefit societies, often related to the chapels and temperance organizations and offering a degree of self-government, were more attractive; though the Reverend Henry Knight, rector of Neath, was not impressed. 'A dread of the new Poor Law,' he said, 'has acted as an incitement to a certain degree of thrift by inducing them to form themselves into provident societies, which are very numerous amongst them – the Druids, for instance. But there is no economy of their funds; they spend the larger portion of their money in robes, velvet caps, and long, flowing white beards; resembling more a troop of ancient mummers than in any way approaching the true Druidical costume; and in this ridiculous dress parade the streets and attend Divine service.' Mr Knight would doubtless not have directed the same criticism to those who took part in the flummery of the rites of the City of London, or the processions that attended the opening of the legal terms, or those accompanying the opening of Parliament, which were paid for not by those who enjoyed them, but out of rates and taxes. Nor do the antics of the Druids sound much different from the rituals of Freemasonry, on which they and other such organizations as the Oddfellows, founded in 1810, the Foresters, the Buffaloes and others were based. In fact, the branches, lodges, tents or chapels of the large friendly societies were far outnumbered by local societies based on individual villages or even individual places of work. 'Dignities of office and social pleasures at their meetings,' it was noted in Warwickshire, 'render the societies attractive.' Another inducement was the annual feast, often at Whitsun, of the kind mentioned earlier. The ostensible objects of the societies or 'field clubs', as they were known in the Midlands, were to provide for medical attention, death and sometimes birth grants, sick pay, and benefits for widows and orphans. Unfortunately the benefits

promised where so generous that the promise could not be ful-
filled, so that many local societies broke up. In at least one case a
society ran a self-supporting dispensary, which would have been a
useful antidote to the amount of quack medicine being sold in
mining areas, but this had to close down after a three-year struggle.
There was, of course, a good deal of scope for losses through
incompetence or fraud, and many societies set up for more
laudable purposes degenerated into mere 'goose clubs' which
redistributed their funds at Christmas in time for the traditional
two-week binge spanning New and Old Christmas Day (25
December to 6 January). By the time effective legislation was
introduced, in 1846, to regulate the affairs of friendly societies, the
'local' element, at any rate, of the movement had begun to lose
credibility, and more interest and reliability were to be found in the
Cooperative movement and in building societies, especially those
building societies of the temporary kind formed to carry out one
specific housing project, which would today be called self-build
associations. In parts of the South Wales coalfield these 'building
clubs' were a significant force in house development round about
the end of the nineteenth century. Their success was due largely to
the fact that the colliers were able to call on the help of local
business and professional worthies to help with organization and,
more important, to guarantee their loans at the bank. It is greatly to
the discredit of the coalmasters and the coalowning gentry of the
mid-nineteenth century, who affected concern for the thrift of the
lower orders, that they did not contribute to the Friendly Society
movement the management and entrepreneurial skills that they
demonstrated in the running of the pits. Their neglect of this not
very onerous duty led the colliers straight into the arms of the
industrial insurance companies, which battened, like the owners,
the butties, the tommy-shop men and the manufacturers of quack
medicine and cheap drink, on a section of the population least able
to take care of itself. It is for this reason that the virtues of the few
enlightened managers, like James Allan of Govan, stand out in such
sharp relief.

5

FIVE PENCE A LIFE

On 19 April 1841, a boy called Robert Cooper, maybe nine, maybe younger, was trapping in the Bensham Seam some 850 feet down at Willington Colliery on Tyneside. About the middle of the day he left his door, propping it open, and went a few yards to play, or perhaps share a bite to eat, with another trapper, Robert Pearson.

At a quarter past one George Campbell, a putter, was returning with an empty wagon from the shaft, heading for the working face and lighting his way with a candle. As he reached the point opposite the passage where Robert Cooper's door was propped open, there was an explosion. George Campbell and the two trappers must have been killed instantly. In the fire that raged through the headways, 160 yards to the north and about the same distance to the west, another twenty-nine men and boys died. John Hall and Robert Campbell were burned and then buried under a fall of stone. Thomas Wood and Joseph Johnson, hewers, were at the face when the blast happened. They ran for the shaft, but were overpowered by gas before they had covered more than a hundred yards, Johnson stuffing his cap in his mouth in a vain effort to stay alive. The blast raced on, dashing wagons to pieces, tossing men about like rag dolls, lifting the cage at the head of the shaft several feet into the air. The fire set alight the stables at the pit bottom and began to burn the coal itself. It was not until two o'clock the following morning that the fire was brought under control, and the bodies were still being brought out two days after that.

Sixteen-year-old George Chalton was working about 500 yards to the east of the shaft at the time of the explosion, helping two men to lay down a new length of tramway. He 'felt a strong wind, and a good deal of dust with it,' he remembered later, and 'knew directly that it was an explosion.' The three of them made for the shaft in the dark, their lights having been blown out. They struggled over falls of rock, and George Chalton fell down four or five times from the effects of the gas, feeling 'as if he was dead asleep, and as if the power of his legs was taken from him'. Their way became lighter: they were coming to the stables, already well alight. Reaching the pit bottom, they found the cage jammed by fallen rock. Another cage was sent down, but they had to climb twelve feet or so up the shaft to reach it. They were the only ones to escape from the pit unhurt.

No one can tell how many men, women and children have been killed or maimed in British pits; but taking the going rate of over 1000 deaths a year in the nineteenth century and the early years of this, a death toll of 250,000 would not be a wild overestimate. As for injuries resulting in more than seven days' absence from work, these were running at over 150,000 a year just before the 1914–18 war. In the context of figures like this, the Willington explosion, with its thirty-two deaths, was a relatively minor incident, and the only reason why such a detailed account of it can be given is that a government inspector, collecting evidence for a Royal Commission, happened to be in the area at the time and went down the pit shortly after the accident, collecting statements from the colliery manager and, among others, George Chalton. Considering that four of the victims were boys of nine, and four others were between ten and thirteen, and that some colliers must have lost friends or relatives or even their families' chief breadwinners, it might have been expected that the disaster would have figured prominently in conversation a fortnight later; but of thirty-eight people who worked underground at Willington and who were interviewed about two weeks afterwards only one, George Chalton, mentioned it. Although he clearly relished having a tale to tell, he did not seem particularly distressed about it, and indeed reckoned, despite his experience, that working in the pit 'agreed with him'.

The Chief Constable of Oldham had something to say about the collier communities' attitude to the toll of pit work. 'There is a great amount of rude callousness on the subject of accidents,' he said. 'In a day or two's time, among such people, even their wives and children seem to have forgotten it. They will say at the time, "Oh, I am not a bit surprised; I expected it – I expected it"; and it soon passes by. There are so many killed, that it becomes quite customary to expect such things. The chiefest talk is just at the moment, until the body gets home, and then there is no more talk about it.' According to the Chief Constable, the effect of a collier's death on *non*-mining sectors of the community was even more relaxed: 'People generally feel, "Oh, it's only a collier!" There would be more feeling a hundred times if a policeman were to kill a dog in the street. In different neighbourhoods here there would be more bother and talk about killing a dog than killing a collier.'

In Scotland a collier's death was an excuse for a debased form of wake, a doctor reported: 'The neighbours usually congregate in numbers in the house, when the whisky bottle is produced; and although it may not follow that they get intoxicated in that house, still it being a beginning leads them on either to adjourn to the public house, and there keep up a constant drinking for two or three days, or else they go to the other houses, and getting a dram at each finish the day in a state of beastly inebriety.'

Even in the relatively God-fearing west Midlands colliers' funerals had a touch of carnival about them. Eighteen-year-old William Troughton reported on the custom in Staffordshire: 'All the men of the pit attend the funeral of a man who has been killed, and the butty finds them in bread and cheese and drink; and they generally get very freshish before they leave.'

It suited everyone, of course, that not too much fuss should be made about pit accidents. Expressions of grief or concern, or inquiries into causes, might stimulate demands for expensive improvements in equipment or alterations in working practices. Fairly consistently, owners and managers tended to defend the way things were done in their own pits, in the face of all evidence and logic, and to blame accidents on wilful breaking of the colliery rules. Thus the cause of the Willington explosion was seen to be the disobedience of the trapper, Robert Cooper, and not the negligent practice of entrusting men's lives to the conscientiousness of a small boy in the last hour of a twelve-hour shift. 'Carelessness' was the cause of accidents most commonly named by management, when it had to discuss them at all, which it preferred not to do. In 1767, the *Newcastle Journal* was obliged by pressure from the Duke of Northumberland, whose income from coal about that time was said to be £10,000 a year, to restrain itself from drawing attention to pit accidents. 'As we are requested to take no particular notice of these things, which, in fact, could have very little good tendency,' the editor, no fearless journalist he, wrote, 'we drop the further mentioning of it.' Until 1814, it was thought superfluous to hold inquests into deaths due to pit accidents since these were so commonplace, and even after that date inquests were often fairly perfunctory. In South Wales it was the practice in the 1840s for the coroner not to bother to hold inquests until there were five or six cases to be disposed of, permits for burial being issued through local constables. In 1841, the coroner at Whitehaven in Cumberland, a Mr Hodgson, took a very calm view of the pit accidents for which the area was notorious, and had been for a century, and saw no necessity to do more than send in a return of fatalities once a quarter to the justices. There was no point in calling for postmortems on accident victims, he said, 'for in most cases the person is killed on the spot, especially when it happens, which is the case in most instances, by the roof of the pit falling on the miner. We have experienced, but not recently, dreadful loss of life by the explosion of inflammable air, but most frequently no one survives to give any account of how the melancholy event occurred.' This was simply not true, for as the amount of detail gathered on the Willington explosion, of which only a small fraction is quoted at the beginning of this chapter, shows, the interest of a government officer – even one with no enforcing powers – could be an admirable spur to investigations. Coroners had, if they wished to use them, considerable powers, though of course they owed their appointments to a hierarchy at the head of which stood the coalowning class. There was certainly resistance to postmortems from the families of victims, but coroners were in a position to overcome this. As a result of this particular neglect, interested doctors in mining areas had no opportunity to build up experience of the nature of internal injuries or even to make accurate judgements of the cause of death.

In Scotland, where the office of coroner did not (and still does not) exist, the investigation of cases of sudden death was the responsibility of procurators fiscal, but in practice such investigations were carried out only if murder or manslaughter were suspected, and not always even then. In 1841 Jane Patterson, a 17-year-old putter at a pit near Tillicoultry in Clackmannanshire, told the government inspector that her father had been 'brought home dead a few years since. He was supposed to have been murdered,' she added, 'but no one sought after those who killed him.' John Baxter's father, too, was murdered, in Bathgate. 'He was thrown into the canal,' John said, 'and the murderer was never sought after, as there was no talk about the death and therefore no inquiry.' As far as pit deaths were concerned, Robert Rodger, joint procurator fiscal for Renfrewshire, doubted whether public inquiries would be worthwhile, and 'in many instances the publicity given to the case by a judicial inquiry would be extremely painful and repugnant to the feelings'. Glasgow's fiscal, George Salmond, had his doubts about instituting the inquest in Scotland for a reason which seems peculiarly appropriate for a Scottish lawyer: 'The chief obstacle would be, as it always has been,' he wrote wearily, 'to get money to remunerate the informer and witnesses, the jurors, etc., etc.' But even when the due process of Scottish law could be trundled into action, it was not always very effective. There was a case at Alloa Colliery round about 1830, when a miner was overwound at the pithead and was killed. The sheriff was called in but, according to a witness, 'after looking at the ropes and examining their strength, he walked away, and no further notice was taken. This is the common practice.' Even this token piece of investigation was pointless, because there is no possible connection between overwinding – failing to stop the winding rope at the appropriate point so that men are either carried up into the wheel or crash to the pit bottom – and the strength or even the condition of the ropes. Overwinding is entirely a matter of human error. For the most part in Scotland, however, it was a case of keeping no records and making no reports. That way, owners and managers were spared embarrassment and the fiscals were saved tedious work.

It is interesting to compare the attitude of Parliament and government to mining casualties with that to railway accidents. The toll of the pits began to rise steeply after the Newcomen engine began to be installed round about the end of the seventeenth century, making possible the working of deeper seams. In the northeast of England, for example, there were, between 1767 and 1815, at least seven major pit explosions each resulting in more than thirty deaths, and between 1815 and 1840 another twelve, not to mention countless smaller tragedies of which no record remains. Nonetheless, it was not until 1835, after almost a century and a half of wholesale slaughter – according to one count, 600 miners in northeast England alone were killed in a two-year period at the beginning of the nineteenth century – that Parliament first inquired into mining safety, and it was another fifteen years after that before the first timid safety requirements were imposed. Colliers were politically of no account; accidents happened to them in areas which were not exposed to public view, and in circumstances where the eyes of gentlefolk would not be offended. By contrast, it took only fifteen years from the opening of the Stockton and Darlington Railway to establish a permanent railways inspectorate. Passenger traffic was from the first designed for the carriage trade; railway accidents could, and did, happen anywhere, sometimes in embarrassingly public circumstances. No doubt an important factor in the establishment of the railway inspectorate in 1840 was the unfortunate death ten years earlier, at the gala opening of the Liverpool and Manchester Railway, of William Huskisson, an MP and former senior cabinet minister, who was so overcome at having his hand shaken by the Duke of Wellington, from whom he had become estranged, that he fell under the wheels of *The Rocket*. Clearly, if railways were to threaten the lives of those in public life, their safety must be closely regulated. Nothing illustrates the significance of the railways inspectorate more clearly than the fact that, two years after its establishment, Queen Victoria made her first tremulous train journey from Slough to Paddington, thus inaugurating the long love affair between the British Royal Family and the railways. It was not until 1912 that George V became the first British monarch to venture down a coal pit.

The comparison is not an idle one. From the beginning, the railway inspectors – who were recruited from the Royal Engineers and were therefore independent – had to inspect and approve lines before opening to the public, and to investigate and report on accidents. This was ten years before it became obligatory even to report, leave alone investigate, pit accidents involving injury, and even then the law required several reinforcing Acts before it stuck. As for the compulsory inspection of pits, this was also introduced in 1850, but as there was a force of only seven inspectors to cover over 3000 collieries the department could hardly be regarded as adequately staffed. The result was that, whereas the regulation of the railways quickly built up a body of knowledge on safety matters and stimulated the invention and installation of new safety devices, that of coal mines proceeded only slowly and with opposition from every quarter. By 1840, in his first report, the chief inspector of railways was already making recommendations for the greater safety of passengers, and in some detail; one conclusion that year, for example, concerned the adoption of London time throughout the system in order to prevent accidents arising from the use of 'local time' on lines where trains were kept apart by the time interval system. In the 1870s, the mines inspectorate was still fighting for regulations to control the use of explosives underground.

Such attentions as there were to the safety of colliers were given, before the mid-nineteenth century, largely by philanthropists from outside the industry, and it was unfortunate that the one supposed improvement that came about in this way backfired badly, resulting in worse working conditions and more accidents. Schoolchildren still learn about the Davy safety lamp because it illustrates an important scientific principle, and the invention earned Davy his baronetcy, but less than twenty years had passed after its introduction in 1816 when it was agreed that, so far from increasing safety in the pits, it had diminished it. By that time, however, the damage had been done and the industry was committed to the lamp.

Davy was an industrial chemist who had not hitherto had any involvement with mining. The story of his invention began with a pit explosion at Felling, near Gateshead, in 1812, in which ninety-two colliers died. Defying the wishes of the Felling owners, the vicar of Jarrow, the Reverend John Hodgson, wrote and published an account of the disaster which caught the eye of a brother parson, the rector of Bishopwearmouth, and a South Shields wine merchant, James Mather. The result was the formation of a society to investigate safety measures in pits, and an invitation from the association to Davy to consider the problem of safely illuminating gassy pits. By coincidence, George Stephenson was experimenting with the same objective at Killingworth Colliery, near Newcastle, and the two men came up with similar solutions. Davy's was the now-familiar lamp with a body of wire gauze which conducts heat away from the flame and prevents it from igniting any surrounding gas; it could also be used as a testing device, since the flame turned blue and elongated in the presence of gas. It is not clear why Davy's name should have become so firmly attached to the safety lamp, unless it was that his connections were more distinguished than those of George Stephenson, then only a colliery mechanic and still some ten years away from national fame.

It was honourable of Davy to renounce any right to royalties on his invention, but in view of subsequent history it is hard to avoid a cynical smile at the news that the coalowners of Newcastle presented him, in 1817, with a dinner service of silver plate in honour of his achievement (and, even-handedly, Stephenson, in the following year, with a silver tankard containing one thousand guineas). These were small prices to pay for something that was to inaugurate a period of unprecedented profit, especially in the Newcastle area. Indeed, a letter to Davy from John Buddle, the Duke of Northumberland's agent, written in June 1816, makes it clear that the economic opportunities afforded by the lamp had been recognized from the start. 'I feel peculiar satisfaction,' Buddle wrote, 'in dwelling upon a subject which is of the utmost importance, not only to the great cause of humanity, and to the mining interest of the country, but also to the commercial and manufacturing interests of the United Kingdom; for I am convinced that by the happy intervention of the safe-lamp, large proportions of the coal mines of the empire will be rendered available, which otherwise might have remained inaccessible. . . . It is not necessary that I should enlarge upon the national advantages which must necessarily result from an invention calculated to prolong our supply of mineral coal, because I think them obvious to every reflecting mind.' It is certainly obvious to every reflecting mind where Buddle's priorities lay.

Almost immediately, advantage was taken of the supposed protection afforded by the Davy lamp to sink pits into regions previously thought unacceptably hazardous. Risks to colliers were thus increased on a dramatic scale, and their working conditions, the time they took to reach the working face (for which, since they were on piece rates, they were not paid) and the damage to their health were all affected for the worse. At the depths now being plumbed, the heat was intense; over ninety degrees was fairly commonplace, and in 1825 Northumberland miners alleged that in one pit there was a steady temperature of 130 degrees Fahrenheit, for which the men were given an extra allowance of sixpence a day. Up to 1816, 600 feet was considered a noteworthy depth for a pit in the northeast. The 1820s and 1830s saw the opening, or deepening, in the northeast of England, of Monkwearmouth (over

1500 feet), Jarrow and Hetton (over 1000 feet), and several more over 800 feet. Deeper shafts increased the perils of manriding, and the larger workforces needed to operate the new pits – over 450 at Willington, Seghill and Heaton in Northumberland, for instance – meant that in any explosion casualties would be proportionately high. Hardly had the applause for Davy died away before, at Harraton Row in June 1817, there was an impressive demonstration that his lamp had not rid mining of the danger from exploding gas. It was a common complaint that safety lamps gave insufficient light to work by, and indeed the early models, which had a gauze body with no glass, were fairly dim. As soon as the overman – the foreman – had turned his back, a hewer at Harraton Row lit a candle. In the explosion that followed, he and thirty-seven others died. It goes without saying that the Davy lamp had been introduced without any attempt to educate the men in its use; there is one recorded instance of a management issuing written instructions to all its underground workers, but as so few colliers could read at all effectively this was perhaps only a gesture. It was common for a miner to open a lamp to light his pipe, for at this period, although individual colliery regulations might prohibit smoking underground, there was no means of enforcement and no general inspection for smoking materials before going below, as is now mandatory. The later regulations governing the use of safety lamps, in force until oil lamps were finally abandoned, were a belated reflection of the hazards of the early days. The lamp was, from the early years of this century, completely enclosed, lockable (the key being left above ground in the lamproom) and inspected for damage after each shift.

For all its faults, the Davy lamp became an indispensable tool of the British collier, and in one of the industry's peak years, 1912, there were nearly 750,000 in use. The lamp became virtually a badge of office; it could be numbered, its number registered against the name of its holder, and in this way, if the worst happened, it could help in the assembly of the grim statistics of a disaster, as will be seen in chapter 8. But in the years following its introduction it was certainly working against rather than for safety. 'Our colliers have adopted [the lamp] with the greatest eagerness,' John Buddle wrote to Davy, but this was at the start. Twenty years later, views had altered. 'None of the men will work with Davy's lamp if they can help it,' reported an overman at the Soap House pit in Sheffield. 'Candles give ten times better light and are much more handy for sticking about in holes and places where they may be wanted,' he went on. 'I think the Davy lamps do more harm than good,' said an overman at Elsecar Colliery, between Rotherham and Barnsley. 'They are sometimes used to save the trouble of proper ventilation which ought always to be adopted as a preservative against the firedamp.' But it was left to a Yorkshire magistrate, John Thorneley, to put his finger on the fundamental error of over-reliance on the Davy lamp: 'When it is used, an explosion may be produced by the imprudence of a single individual.' Mr Thorneley quoted an instance when two boys were given lamps to take to the men in the workings. The careful instructions they were given excited their curiosity, and on the way they sat down to look at the lamps more closely. ' "Eh!" said one of the boys, "See what a flame there is!", and they at length opened it to take the light out, when explosion immediately ensued.' Attempts to prevent interference with Davy lamps were made quite early on in the North of England; but 'the men ingeniously contrived to poke holes with great nails on both sides of the gauze in order to blow the flame through, and light their pipes'. The workforce of a whole pit could be put at risk by the occasional obstreperous collier who declared that 'he was not paid for working with Davy's lamp'. There were, of course, bloody-minded and careless and stupid men at work in the pits before the lamp was introduced – for example, it was a common sport in Midlands pits to 'play with wildfire', as firedamp was called there, breathing some in and then lighting it like a flare as it was slowly exhaled – but the opportunity provided by the lamp to work in more dangerous seams enhanced the consequences of folly. In Northumberland and Durham there were, between 1817 and 1841, 109 pit accidents resulting in death. (This was a figure arrived at not from official sources, since there were none, but from a painstaking combing of local newspapers by James Mather, the philanthropic wine merchant of South Shields, so it may not be entirely accurate.) Of these, fifty-eight were explosions of gas, but they accounted for about four fifths of the 919 deaths during that period. As late as the 1930s, as we shall see in the last chapter, gas could still claim over 250 lives at a time.

One thing that emerged once lists of explosions began to be compiled (and that could have been discovered earlier if records had been kept), was that it was possible to name high-risk periods for gassy pits. For example, an unusually high proportion of explosions took place on Mondays or, in pits where 'Saint Monday' was observed, Tuesdays. If it had been noticed earlier, this would have pointed to the importance of keeping ventilation going on Sundays even though there was no hewing. Similarly, it was established by the 1840s that the incidence of explosions was related to atmospheric changes. Of seventy-one explosions in Northumberland and Durham, it was noted, almost half had taken place in the months of September, October and November, and one third in the months of June, July and August. Winter was the safest time from this point of view. Given this information, it would not have been difficult to devise a warning system based on continuous barometric readings. Nothing was done, however, and throughout the nineteenth century and into our own, September and October continued to be the months in which you were most likely to open your newspaper and read about some hideous firestorm in a pit.

Another area in which the fecklessness of colliery managements was almost incredible was in the matter of keeping accurate plans, an omission that led to at least two major disasters, and many minor ones, in the years before 1850, when the obligation to keep plans was introduced; though, of course, in the absence of pre-1850 plans the danger persisted. On 3 May 1815, new workings were being explored at Heaton, near Newcastle, and the colliers broke through into the worked-out galleries of an older pit. Flood water rushed through, drowning a number of colliers variously estimated at between seventy-five and ninety. 'Some miraculous escapes were made,' says an account of 1869, 'by some of the persons who happened to be close to the shaft, but the place where the water burst in being many hundred yards distant, and forming a descending plane of one in ten, the tremendous force of the current bore down every obstacle, and hurled in the most awful confusion men, horses, carriages and all that stood in its way towards the shaft, where some fortunate beings escaped when the water was nearly breast high. Many months elapsed before the waters were sufficiently drained to render the workings again accessible.' Fifty-four bodies were brought out the following February, 'and were all recognized with one exception, principally by their clothes'. It was clear that the trapped men had taken a long time to die, during which they had fed off their horses, candles, and even the bark from the pit props. One man, it was thought, had not been dead long when the recovery party arrived.

Horrifying though the Heaton disaster was, it was at least, according to the state of mining regulations at the time, unpredictable. A similar flooding at Workington in Cumberland in 1837 was the result of wilful risk-taking by the colliery manager. The Workington shafts were on the seashore and the seam they worked extended under the sea for over a mile, steadily rising towards the seabed. 'Although the pillars of coal which had been left to support the overlying strata were barely large enough to afford the necessary support to the roof,' says one report, 'the manager, in his anxiety to produce a large quantity of coal, proceeded in a reckless manner to reduce them still further in size by working them partly away.' Eventually, on the rising seam, coal was being worked only ninety feet below the seabed; the safe minimum was reckoned to be 360 feet, perhaps more according to the nature of the overlying strata, and this, of course, was on the assumption that adequate pillars had been left. Early in 1837, there began to be heavy roof falls, accompanied by discharges of salt water; some men said they had heard the sound of the sea above them; trickles of sand appeared in the workings. An overman, William Thornton, reported all this to the manager, Coxton, and warned him that the sea might break in. Thornton was dismissed. Some men left the pit, and others were persuaded to stay only by the offer of extra money. The Reverend Henry Curwen, son of the colliery proprietor, heard the rumours that 'the pit would be lost if we continued working it for three weeks'. He consulted his mother, but they decided that it was only a rumour. However, it was not. On 30 July 1837, the sea broke in, drowning thirty-six men. 'A black gurgling whirlpool,' it was reported, 'for some time marked the aperture and the entrance of the waters at a considerable distance from the shore.' Dr Dickenson, who happened to be standing on shore near a ventilation shaft, had his hat blown off. The bodies of the victims were not recovered. Coxton, the manager, fled into hiding; otherwise, it was said, he would have been torn limb from limb 'could he have been found by the heart-rent assemblage of the relatives of the sufferers who thronged to the spot'. As it was, his only punishment was dismissal, and it was generally agreed, at least by the pillars of the community, that he should be the scapegoat, though there is some suspicion of pressure on this score. One local doctor, employed by the colliery and questioned about the disaster, refused to give any evidence when he heard it would be printed; and this was four years after the event. Another – Dr Dickenson – thought that no blame could be attached to anyone but Coxton. 'A more humane man than Mr Curwen does not exist,' he said, with more than a suggestion of reading from a prepared statement. 'He had no idea of there being danger, I am sure, for though reports had reached him, they were not such as he could rely on.' The Reverend Henry Curwen, however, was satisfied that his father had received no warning 'as to the liability of an irruption of the sea'. But these were very muddy waters altogether. Mr Curwen senior appears to have been absent from home when the rumours were being heard, for otherwise why should his son have discussed them with Mrs Curwen? And if Mr Curwen had received no warning, this must surely have been his son's fault, since *he* had. And eyebrows might well be raised when it was learned that a decision on the safety of a pit – which was clearly a high risk one in any case – was left to a parson and his mother, who surely cannot have been qualified to take it. There was also the nasty business of William Thornton's dismissal. But the Curwens managed to survive all these questions, because there was no mechanism for asking them.

The Workington disaster pointed to two issues: the accurate planning of proposed mine workings, which became obligatory thirteen years later although in practice it did not become fully effective until 1919; and the qualifications of colliery managers, which were to wait until 1872 before receiving the attention of Parliament. Coxton had, according to his employer Curwen, been hired on the strength of one reference, half what most ladies of the time would have called for if they were engaging a kitchen maid.

Accidents (if that is the word) on the scale of Workington, Heaton, and the larger culls of Lord Firedamp produced some reaction, if only local, muted and temporary. But most of those underground in the eighteenth and nineteenth centuries were at risk not from the dramatic disaster, but from the steady chop, chop of everyday mishaps. At Holmfirth in Yorkshire, 10-year-old Enoch Hurst was killed by a piece of coal falling from a corf in the shaft as he was waiting to go up. No blame was attached to the owners; it was reckoned that he should have got out of the way. At Allerton, Joshua Stansfield, eight, accidentally fell down the shaft; but then he was said to be 'not very sharp'. William Smith, ten, of Pinxton in Derbyshire, was killed when a thirty-hundredweight stone fell on him. At Tupton, 14-year-old George Goodhall was in the habit of hanging on to the chain with one hand when going up or down the shaft. One day he lost his hold and was killed. Joseph Halliwell died at Flockton when the roof fell in on him. At Cumbernauld, Robert Russell died when he was run over by an underground wagon. He was thirteen. At Alloa, John Patterson was overwound. William Phelp fell from the winding rope at the Elgin Colliery, Dunfermline, when a piece of rock struck him. Four men were killed at Cowpen, north of Newcastle, when they were repairing the lining of a shaft. Some loose timber hit their scaffold, which collapsed and fell with them nearly 600 feet to the pit bottom. At Hetton, a boy fell asleep on the wagonway and was run over; another, driving a horse wagon, went to sleep, fell off, and went under its wheels. At Greasley in Derbyshire, a 17-year-old youth waiting his turn to go below slipped on the ice at the unguarded pithead, and fell to his death. Four were killed at Paulton, in Somerset, in 1830 when a winding rope broke. Not far away, at Wellsway Colliery, Radstock, twelve men died in 1839 when the rope snapped as they were about to go down. 'The rope,' according to a gravestone in Midsomer Norton churchyard, 'was generally believed to have been maliciously cut.' In 1899, again at Wellsway, the cage was lowered into almost boiling water, and a man in it was scalded to death.

It seems insane that, as late as 1899, there should be near-boiling water at the bottom of the pit shaft, with nothing to prevent a cage being wound down into it, but this was nothing like as reckless as the winding practices of earlier years. Whatever the system of paying for work underground, the expense of winding men and coal up and down the shaft, and the maintenance of the shaft itself, always fell on the coalmasters. These were obligations that had no relation to profit or productivity, and so they tended to be discharged as cheaply as possible. The cheapest form of manriding, common in the eighteenth century, was for each collier to hold on to a loop in the rope, using his free hand to fend him off the sides of the shaft. A refinement of this – in use well into the nineteenth century – was to provide a chain into which each collier put his legs, again leaving him with a free hand to protect himself from injury against the shaft sides. Sometimes boys would sit astride the knees of the men, or alternatively would cling to the rope with their hands, twining their legs around it. Yet another method was for the men to sit on laths of wood bound into the rope, or on the crosslatch, the beam at the end of the rope to which the corves were hitched. In other pits, colliers rode up and down in the corves themselves; a corf of men might be going down while one of coal came up, and as outside the northeast it was rare for any division in the shaft to be provided, or for the corves to be fitted with guides, collisions were frequent. When this happened, either the passengers, or some of them, would be tipped out, or the coal would be tipped out and fall on the passengers as they continued downwards. In the northeast this danger was avoided by bratticing the shaft – separating the upward and downward courses by shuttering – which was also a useful means of providing through ventilation without the expense of a second shaft.

The shaft itself presented further hazards. Stray bits of timber were sometimes left at the sides, eventually working loose and snagging the rope. On the borders of Lancashire and Cheshire, shafts were lined with brick – not always mortared – only as far as the nearest hard rock. As the workings proceeded, subsidence could loosen bricks and rock, sending them hurtling to the pit bottom. It was rare for owners to have the forethought, as had those of the Moira Bath pit in Leicestershire, to fit a solid iron bonnet, or 'umbrella' as they called it there, over the chain so that those going up or down were protected from anything falling from above. Where the men rode up and down in corves, these could be dangerously overcrowded, especially at the end of a shift. There was an instance of a collier who rushed to be twelfth man in an already overcrowded corf, but it pulled away as he reached it. As he stood waiting for the next, 'eleven corpses were scattered at his feet'. Of one hundred pit deaths reported in south Staffordshire in 1838, twenty-eight were from accidents in the shafts, only roof falls killing more. Few owners operated such good practice as was reported at Snibston in Leicestershire, where there was a man on duty at both top and bottom of the shaft to make sure that no more than four men or five or six boys, according to size, went up or down at any one time. As for signalling when corves were on the move – quite feasible, practically speaking, by 1800 – the best usual practice was a cry of 'Hold out' from top or bottom, which might or might not be heard.

Then, of course, there was the question of the condition of the ropes or chains. Ropes were generally preferred, for at least any faults in them could be detected by inspection and soon became obvious; chains were apt to snap suddenly and unexpectedly, especially in frosty weather or if they had been given an unnoticed blow; but, of course, they lasted longer and were more easily repaired, so they were popular with masters. Most favoured by colliers was the flat rope, composed of four strands sewn side by side. It would be extremely bad luck if all four strands were to part at once – though it happened – and flat ropes were less likely to fly off the pulley. They came into fairly general use in the 1830s and 1840s. The wire hawser was, of course, several decades into the future.

Until the eighteenth century and in some places well into Victorian times, power for manriding and coal haulage up the shaft was provided by horse gins – using horses described by one witness as 'of the worst description, wind-galled, spavined and blind' – or even by human muscle-power. Increasingly, however, this work was taken over by engines, and this introduced the hazard of overwinding. It was always caused by the inattention of the engineman, or, more often, in Lancashire and Derbyshire, the engineboy. In the 1850s, for example, the engineman at Withy Mills pit in Somerset came on shift drunk and overwound nine men into the wheel. They came off like monkeys, said a contemporary account. Near Halifax a boy, David Pellett, was overwound by his own uncle and grandfather, whose attention had been distracted by a passing funeral. But the majority of engine minders were boys, sometimes as young as ten or eleven, who were cheap to employ. How conscientious or capable they were was critical to everyone ascending or descending, whose lives depended on the speed of the engine, its behaviour (and many were erratic), and the boy's judgement of when to stop. Bits of rag might be tied to the ropes to mark the top and bottom limits of travel, but these could wear away and, especially on the downward trip, it was generally hit-or-miss. The upward journey was enlivened by the knowledge that to be overdrawn meant almost certain death, or at best serious injury. At Morley Park in Derbyshire, the engineboy left his post and three men and boys were overdrawn. A 13-year-old was killed. One of the men lost an arm, the other had a broken leg. It was generally agreed among hewers that it was a scandal to employ 'little bits of lads' for this work. One hewer, James Warrener of Oldham, was once let down the shaft by a boy he had beaten the night before: 'He let the tub in which I was go down at such a rate that the wheels were broken, and I saved myself only by running up as much of the loose rope with my hands as I could.'

It was at the Robin Hood pit, near Oldham, that 10-year-old James Taylor – or Lump Lad, as they called him in the pit – had a narrow squeak. He was waiting at the pit bottom to be drawn up and had knocked at the sounding rod for a tub to be let down, when a man who had been overwound fell down the pit, almost on top of him. The man was dead before he landed. The engineman ran away home, but the master fetched him back and he continued winding for the rest of the day. He was still winding, a year later, at another pit. In fact, the certainty of a fatal fall down the shaft after overwinding was entirely preventable. By 1840, a self-acting trapdoor to close the mouth of the pit had been devised, and was in operation in the Barnsley and Bradford areas. It was no longer necessary to make a grab for corves or colliers as they arrived at the top of the shaft.

By the 1860s, manriding in loops on the rope, the sight of which reminded one observer of a string of onions and another of a chandelier, 'the resemblance being rendered in this instance the more close by each [man] holding a lighted candle in his hand', was dying out except in shallow pits. The use of some kind of container for the colliers did not, however, end the danger of overwinding, as was shown at Hayeswood Colliery in Somerset in 1845, when an inattentive engineman overwound seven men, corf and all. All were badly hurt, but all survived, so that it was perhaps better, if you were going to be overwound, to be inside something rather than simply hanging on to the rope. It took legislation, in 1855, to enforce the obvious safety precaution of providing an indicator to show the position of the cage in the shaft, and a means of signalling between top and bottom. However, legislation isn't everything, and as late as 1913 there were sixteen deaths and forty-eight injuries from overwinding. Even in 1944, it was possible for six men to be injured through overwinding at Pensford in Somerset; it turned out that the indicator and overwinding check had been disconnected for some reason to do with the wartime blackout.

For the reasons mentioned earlier, it was difficult to persuade owners to invest in new manriding equipment. The cage was the subject of experiments in the northeast before 1820, but it was slow to be adopted. Even slower was a cage so designed that colliers could not fall out of it or be injured by obstructions in the shaft. In 1862 a cage incorporating a fail-safe device similar to that used in modern lifts was on view at the Paris Exhibition, and by the end of the decade had become virtually compulsory in French pits. (The French had devised an ingenious licensing system which imposed such burdens on owners who had not fitted safety equipment that they were effectively driven out of business.) A group of British owners visiting the exhibition, however, was not impressed. The owners were concerned at the need for constant inspection, and maybe replacement, of the spring which was the essential feature of the fail-safe mechanism, and then they fell back on the hardy annual of all owners' objections to safety improvements: they feared (they said) that the apparatus would have a 'tendency to make people careless about the examination and renewal of ropes', ignoring the fact (or missing the point) that if the system failed safe the condition of the ropes would be less critical.

It was a common argument among owners that improvements were being rejected not because of the expense but for their colliers' own good. To read the submissions of owners to the Children's Employment Commission, for example, you would believe that there was nothing the owners would like better than to relieve little mites from the toils of trapping; but, alas, their parents wanted work for them, and trapping was essentially a job for small people who wouldn't get in the way of the corves (or who, if they did, were expendable). In fact, nothing would have been simpler than to do away with the need for trappers by fitting two-way swing doors, or to adopt one of two automatic systems invented by an ingenious mechanical parson, the Reverend John Blackburn of Attercliffe, Sheffield. 'Either of them would succeed,' Mr Blackburn wrote in 1841, adding sadly, 'but I have no expectation of their being adopted: the love of money is so strong it overcomes natural affection; yet the gain to parents by boys is confessedly small.' It was true that improvements were not always welcomed by colliers, who were suspicious of change and were in few cases overcome by natural affection for their children. But in their conservatism the men had allies in the coalmasters, whose reasons were quite different. Robert Clarke, master at Silkstone Colliery near Barnsley, was told about Mr Blackburn's ideas. 'I object to any species of machinery for the purpose,' he retorted, 'because I am sure it would not be secure, and when it got wrong the hurriers could not be trusted to give notice.' (It is this kind of objection that makes the eager adoption of the Davy lamp suspect. The traditional coalmaster's attitude would have been that it would make people careless. Perhaps the productivity, rather than the safety, aspects had been Davy's main sales pitch.)

Mr Clarke and his fellow masters were running the pits in just about the best way they could be run, but if they baulked at such a relatively inexpensive matter as the fitting of automatic trapdoors, it may be imagined how much resistance there was to the idea of guaranteeing an escape route in case a pit's main shaft was obstructed. It was not until 1862 that owners were persuaded by law to provide two separate outlets, as a result of a disaster at Hartley Colliery near Newcastle which was almost certainly the worst in Britain from any cause other than explosion.

The toll of this accident – 204 deaths – was out of all proportion to its beginnings, and it is fairly rare among mining disasters in truly justifying the term 'accident'. No one could have foreseen that the cast-iron beam of the pumping engine was about to break, or that when it did it should fall down the shaft, or that eight men should happen to be coming up in the cage at the time, or that the collision between the beam and the cage should have sent the forty-ton piece of iron spinning down the shaft, taking lumps of rock and bits of timber down about 400 feet with it. Three of the men in the cage survived, but the mass of debris at the pit bottom trapped 199 men and boys. Their situation was hopeless from the start, because they had to share what air there was with a number of well-fuelled ventilating furnaces; but it became clear when their bodies were eventually reached that they had made some attempt to force a way out. Newly sawn timbers were found, and indeed the sounds of activity had been heard by the rescuers above. There was a suggestion later that the rescue attempt was badly organized, and that if things had moved faster the trapped men might have been reached in time. The peculiar horror of Hartley was the slow death of the victims; however destructive an explosion might be, it was over quickly. Suggestions at the subsequent inquiry that every pit should have two separate shafts were, however, strongly resisted. It would be impossible and unjust, it was said, to impose such a requirement. The state had no right to interfere to such a degree with private industry. Furthermore, many pits would not be able to bear such an expense and would have to close, throwing many colliers out of work. Nonetheless, a Mines Act was passed within the year requiring every pit to have two shafts, a rare example in mining legislation of swift action. In fact, it was a token gesture, since the Hartley accident was the result of a chain of events unlikely to be repeated, and in any case the air remaining below in the event of an accident might well not have been enough to sustain the trapped colliers as they made their way to an alternative shaft. As witnesses to the inquiry had forecast, the new requirement did indeed result in the closure of many older pits, and there was a great weeding-out of unproductive workings in the years following 1862. By contrast, the new law no doubt contributed to the safety of the new generation of collieries, such as the series of exceptionally deep pits sunk in the Castleford and Pontefract areas in the 1870s. To follow the letter of the law was not the end of the matter, however; as late as 1957 it was reported that although New Rock Colliery, near Midsomer Norton in Somerset, had its regulation two shafts, the cage in one of them was so small that if an accident happened to the other it would take six hours to wind up a shift of men.

It would be tedious to follow the wealth of nineteenth-century mining legislation in detail, but it is worth noting that in 1913, 269 more miners died than in 1866, which is no great tribute to its effectiveness. One problem noted by several observers was that Mines Acts tended to be liberally sprinkled with such phrases as 'so far as possible' or 'as far as practicable', easy let-outs for the unscrupulous owner. Another was the inadequate staffing of the mines inspectorate. In 1907, with over 3000 pits to supervise, there were only forty inspectors, and although the strength was doubled to help enforce the greatly expanded requirements of the 1911 Coal Mines Act, inspection could still be no more than superficial. The feebleness of legislation in the face of an owner who set out simply to ignore it was cruelly illustrated in South Wales when, on 14 October 1913, the Universal pit at Senghenydd blew up.

In terms of lives lost – 439 – Senghenydd was the worst disaster on record in British mining. Many aspects of the explosion were to be echoed nearly twenty years later at Gresford, which is examined in some detail in chapter 8, but it can be said here that both owners and managers at Senghenydd had been consistently ignoring, defying or evading safety requirements for years. Despite a panic three years earlier when the pit had to be evacuated, nothing had been done to clear explosive coal dust. The fire which followed the explosion destroyed much of the evidence, but it was thought that the initial spark came from the bare wires of the shaft signalling system, a danger of which all owners had been warned in a Home Office circular some months before. The management had sought, and obtained, extra time in which to put into effect the 1911 Act's requirement on the reversal of the ventilation current (which would, it was thought, have saved about a hundred lives). The Act had come into effect on 1 January 1913. The management had been given until 30 September. But on 14 October, the day of the explosion, no work had been started.

The management came before the local magistrates, who may or may not be suspected of partiality, for these infringements. There were seventeen charges against the manager and four against the company. The four against the company were dismissed on the grounds that the directors had properly appointed a manager and had no knowledge of the offences. Of the charges against the manager, seven were dropped and three dismissed. On the remaining charges the manager was fined a total of twenty-two pounds, or two and a half months. 'Miners' lives at 1s.1¼d each!' the local Labour paper headlined its court report. Actually, it was overgenerous. The exact price was only just over a shilling; five pence a head, as we would say.

6

BONDSMEN AND BUTTIES

Walter Pryde was born on the Prestongrange estate in Midlothian in 1760 into effective slavery. His life and work were literally the property of Lord Prestongrange and, as the law stood then, so too, in due course, would be those of his wife and children. When an estate changed hands by sale or inheritance, its bonded servants passed with it. If the laird had work for Walter Pryde to do, he was bound to do it on the laird's terms; if not, he could be rented to another employer. There was no legal way of escape, unless a release or 'testimonial' could be obtained from the laird, and the law was enforced with rigour. Lairds even had the power to bring back colliers who had enlisted in the army or navy. Absconders might, on their return, be shackled against a wall with their necks locked in iron collars, or – a punishment Walter Pryde saw being carried out many times in his youth – they might be made to 'go the rown', tied at the gin, facing the horse, and running backwards all day.

There was a brisk trade in displaced colliers, who could be moved about at will by the tacksmen, or agents. But bound men in other pits resented the arrival of strangers, and Walter Pryde's grandfather was among a group who were so frightened by the death threats of the colliers at a pit where they were to be sent that they petitioned Lord Prestongrange in 1746 for protection.

Walter himself started work as a coal bearer when he was nine. He lived to see the slavery of colliers in Scotland abolished, and indeed on into a ripe old age, hewing until he was seventy-five, fathering eleven children and marrying a durable wife who, despite eleven births, was still coal bearing at sixty-six.

The bondage of colliers in Scotland was a curious survival of the land system dating from feudal times. By an Act of 1701, most Scotsmen had been freed of their feudal obligations and granted protection from imprisonment without warrant or trial, but the Act specifically excluded colliers and salters. It may seem odd that two such apparently disparate occupations should have been singled out for prejudice, but in fact salt making and coal mining were about Scotland's only pre-Industrial Revolution industries employing large numbers of people, and the link between them was strong since coal was needed for the extraction of salt. Indeed, one of Scotland's oldest pits, at the unlikely site of Brora in east Sutherland, devoted virtually its entire output to the associated saltworks in the early nineteenth century. It is less easy to explain why, at least in Fife, it was usual until the nineteenth century to deny to colliers and salters burial in consecrated ground.

In 1774, a first attempt was made to extend to these two groups the rights gained by other Scots in 1701, but the freedom granted then was so hedged about with conditions and procedures – the collier had to take the initiative, for example, by starting proceedings in the Sheriff's court, which few were equipped to do – that many remained in bondage. For all that, the date of the first emancipation, 3 July 1775, was for many years commemorated in Fife as a holiday, and toasts were drunk to Lord Abercorn, who had steered the 1774 Bill through Parliament. Finally, in 1799, a further Act declared all the remaining bound colliers and salters free.

Proprietors of Scottish coal pits were divided on the wisdom of this break with tradition. Some, taking encouragement from Adam Smith, who had scorned the description of the old bondage as slavery and had pointed out that, unlike slaves, Scottish colliers could own property (by which he meant chattels) and were 'free as to marriage and religion', feared that once they were freemen the colliers would desert the pits for some more congenial occupation, or would go south to Northumberland and Durham, where rapid expansion had created a labour shortage and wage rates were attractively high. Others, including Lord Abercorn, perceived that an expansion of the coal trade in Scotland was coming (indeed, with the opening of the Carron ironworks at Falkirk in 1760, significantly transforming within a few years what had been a cattle-droving station into an industrial centre, it had already come), and that unless bondage could be removed it would be impossible to maintain, leave alone expand, the workforce. They were right in that, and the years following the 1799 Act saw large numbers of immigrants to the Scottish coalfields, notably from Ireland.

From 1799, Scottish colliers were hired on an agreement for one year, with a bounty dependent on good behaviour and regular attendance at work paid at the year's end, but by the 1830s the annual agreement had been replaced in most places by a simpler one allowing for two weeks' – in parts of Fife, six weeks' – notice on either side. As in the West Riding of Yorkshire, hewers were paid an agreed rate for coal delivered at the pit bottom in the case of pits with shafts, or at the surface or the drift mouth in pits (of which there were many in the east of Scotland) to which access was by ladders or turnpike stairs. Hewers provided and paid their own hurriers or bearers. It was clearly an advantage for a hewer to be married, because he could then provide himself with free labour, though it was sometimes possible to take on an orphan or a widow's child – a 'fremd' or 'fremit' bearer – in exchange for only food and clothing. There was an unusual amount of haulage work in the thin seams of Scotland, and this could seriously affect the earnings of a collier without children. For example, at Edmonstone Colliery, in Midlothian, James Ross needed two teenage girls to bear for him, effectively halving his earnings, because he had no wife and children. In the same pit, Agnes Moffatt and her sister, about the same age, worked for their father for nothing. It was not surprising that, as Thomas Moore, the manager of Penston Colliery in East Lothian, remarked, 'Colliers marry here very young.' On the other hand, a family could, by prodigious effort, survive the loss of a father. At Loanhead Colliery, David Burnside was, at twelve, an unusually young hewer. With an older sister and a brother of ten bearing for him, he picked up about one pound a week to support them and their widowed mother.

Another survival in the Scottish coalfields, as well as in Wales and Derbyshire, was the truck system, which flourished in some places quite openly and in others in a concealed form. Truck was repeatedly declared illegal in various nineteenth-century Acts of Parliament, but it proved resistant to the most earnest efforts of legislators. In the coal industry – only one of many where it flourished – it was particularly associated with areas where there were long intervals between paydays, such as North Wales and parts of Scotland, where payment was made once a month. In its purest and original form, truck was the payment of wages in special coinage which could be spent only at company shops, 'tommy shops', where the goods obtainable were often called 'tommy rot'. Since no state could put up with the existence of a rival currency, and since the offence was easily detected, this form of truck was virtually extinct by about 1800, though a surviving remnant was discovered in the west of Scotland in the 1840s. It was not hard, however, given a dependent and fairly feckless workforce, to come up with alternative methods of operating truck, and they all revolved round credit. Between paydays, colliers and their families could get credit at the tommy shop, whose true ownership was, in deference to the law, hazy but was usually closely related to the colliery company, or the manager, or, in the case of some of the Duke of Bridgewater's collieries near Manchester in the eighteenth century, to the landowner, whose tenancy agreements with shopkeepers took into account the likely profits of tommy trade. Since the tommy shop was the only source of credit, it could charge more or less what it liked for goods of very inferior, and often adulterated, quality. In North Wales it was reckoned that it was better to earn seventeen shillings a week at a pit without a tommy shop than twenty shillings with one, and in any case, as one collier said, 'Even if the shop is fair one likes to have one's money to go where one likes with it.' But any collier whose family chose to shop elsewhere, if, given the isolation of many pit villages, this were possible, would soon find himself out of work. Tommy, in this setting, offered a number of ways of maximizing profits. Since there was, in a pit village, no opportunity to compare prices, straightforward profiteering was easy, and in 1817 it was alleged in the House of Lords, a forum not notably sympathetic to the working class, that some miners were being forced to pay double the fair price for flour. Then there was adulteration, a science which reached its highest forms in Victorian Britain. No one knew better than a tommy shopkeeper how much sand could be added to sugar, how much dried elder to tea, how much chalk to flour or how much putty to the bottom of the scale pan without arousing suspicion. Then there was the interest of a penny or twopence in the shilling that could be taken as interest for credit. The finest flowering of truck seems to have been in Glamorgan and Monmouthshire where, it was reported in 1842, there still persisted a custom common in the Duke of Bridgewater's collieries a century before: 'The wages of the working collier are very rarely paid in money, but a shop in the neighbourhood, not professedly in the hands of the proprietors of the works, advances goods to the workmen. . . . The books of the shop and the books of the colliery are checked on the payday at the same office, and the balance, if any, is handed over to the men. It very often happens, however, that the men unfortunately have nothing to receive for months together.' The solution in such cases was for a man to take some goods on tick against the following payday, and trade them in for a drink or even, according to two Welsh schoolmasters, pay with them for their children's lessons. 'Bless you, sir, several of us don't know what money is,' said a 50-year-old collier at Hengoed, where in 1841 the men struck for payment in cash – and won. The tommy system was, of course, particularly hard on wives and children who received no pay in their own right; a whole family might find itself continually working to pay off an increasing mountain of credit. This was one reason why a substantial proportion of the mining population was always on the move, one step ahead, with any luck, of the bailiff.

Although the collier's lot in Northumberland and Durham was in many ways as bad as anywhere else, it was – at any rate by the nineteenth century – not burdened with tommy, and some security of employment was given by the bond, the system of hiring. The annual bond had its origins in the traditional method of binding farm servants and labourers, and the signing ceremony was in many areas accompanied by a feast day comparable with the hiring fairs of rural districts. A writer in 1811 painted a picture of the colliers' turnout for binding day: 'In their dress they often affect to be gaudy, and are fond of clothes of glaring colours; their holiday waistcoats (called by them "posey jackets") are frequently of very curious patterns, displaying flowers of various hues; and their stockings mostly of blue, purple, pink or mixed colours. A great part of them have their hair very long, which on workdays is either tied in a queue, or rolled up in curls; but when dressed in their best attire, it is commonly spread over their shoulders. Some of them wear two or three narrow ribbons round their hats, placed at equal distances, in which it is customary with them to insert one or more bunches of primroses or other flowers.' Another account adds to this pastoral picture an impression of sweetness and light between masters and men about this time. 'The employers,' it says, 'seldom meddled with [the men's] fancies or their quarrels, and the men in return seldom interfered with their masters, to whom they evinced more of the attachment of customary subserviency than is ever now witnessed. . . . The periodical hirings were probably gone through as a mere matter of form, and the hired spent their money and their lives with little knowledge of, and less care for, what was going on in the great world above and around them.' All this makes the coalfields of the northeast sound as if they can surely never have been; but it was true enough that in the late eighteenth and early nineteenth centuries elements of the old rural-based way of life persisted alongside early rumblings of the thunder to come. In 1765 and 1789, miners' strikes in the northeast of England led to machine-breaking at a number of pits; yet employers were still, alongside the bond, observing the custom of arleing – paying each collier at the binding a bounty for each of the sons who was to work with him. At times in the eighteenth century, when labour was short, this could be as much as ten pounds for each son, but by 1811 it had dwindled to a token half-guinea or so, and by 1840 it had died out altogether.

Reflecting its agricultural origins, the colliers' bond ran originally from autumn to autumn, but as this caused a hitch in production at a time of peak sales of coal the term was altered in 1812 to run from April to April. Initially, it was the custom for the clauses of the bond to be read out before the colliers signed it, but this could take some time since by the 1830s the document had increased in complexity and could be several thousands of words long, including detailed terms of payment, instructions on methods of working, colliery regulations and, where colliery housing was provided, as was usual in the northeast, conditions of tenancy. (Glass to be kept in good repair; fourteen days to get out if employment ceased; no dogs to be kept were typical conditions.) It even contained a provision for arbitration in the event of disputes. The bond was couched in such legal language, which submerged itself from time to time into curtains of dependent clauses, that it can have meant little even to those literate colliers able to read it at leisure, and must have meant even less to those who heard it gabbled at top speed. An official present at one signing questioned some of the colliers afterwards about the bond, and 'scarcely one of the witnesses whom I examined could give any outline of the provisions of the agreement to which they had thus formally consented, though well acquainted with the bearing of some stipulations which they considered grievances'. 'Signing' was something of a misnomer, because, regardless of whether a collier could sign his name in script, it had become the practice, for the sake of speed, to make a mark. 'I observed,' the same official reported, 'more than one hundred persons indicate their assent and signature by stretching their hands over the shoulder of the agent and touching the top of his pen while he was affixing the cross to their names, and this, I was told, was a common practice.'

Although the bond gave colliers a measure of security and even contained, in some instances, provisions for short-time working or what would today be called a guaranteed working week, it had a number of drawbacks. Because the demand for labour was variable – a cold snap in London, the northeast's main market, or the not infrequent sinking of a London-bound coaster could result in an unexpected leap in demand – extra short-term help was obtained by taking on unbound men, who might be migrants or men whom former employers had refused to sign again. In Durham in 1841, it was estimated that as much as a quarter of the collier workforce was 'floating'. Although the unbound men were subject to the same conditions as those who had signed the bond, there was always the suspicion that they might, in the event of a dispute, work on regardless or accept a lower rate for the job. Indeed, this often happened, and here lies the germ of the blackleg problem for which the Northumberland and Durham coalfield was, in the latter half of the nineteenth century, to become notorious. The bond was a legal document, and a man who broke its terms lay himself open to fines, dismissal, or, if he left his place of work before he had worked out his time, a term in prison. In the south Durham district in the year 1839–40, 172 men spent periods in Durham jail for various bond offences. Not being under these constraints, the unbound men were resented, and so the bond became associated with the beginnings of trade-union activity, sporadic though this was.

The disadvantage of the annual bond from the points of view of both employer and employed was that it focused the heat of negotiations on one month or less in the year. Until 1812, the autumn signings gave the colliers an advantage, since the pressure of demand was an incentive for the masters to settle. After 1812, with the spring signing, the advantage switched; the masters could bear with a lengthy dispute during the quiet summer months. But, either way, the signing of the bond too easily became an occasion for, on the one hand, a tightening of the screws on colliers or, on the other, the rehearsal of old and new grievances. An early demand from the colliers, in 1826, was that the bond should be available for inspection two weeks in advance of the signing, a call which was resisted. Over 4000 colliers were said to have joined the Association of Colliers on the Rivers Tyne and Wear, which was founded round the bond issue and was the first trade union – short-lived though it was – in British coalfields. Five years later, before the 1831 signing, the Association called a strike for improvements in the terms, and no work was done for two months. Despite calls for good order from the men's leaders, there were a few outbreaks of violence – this was the year after the revolt of farm workers, when barns, ricks, farms and poor-houses had been mobbed and set alight – but the army commander for the North of England reported, after an inspection of the northeast, that the men were 'perfectly peaceable in their behaviour, extremely civil when met with on the road', and that everything was conducted in the most orderly manner.

This pleasing and tolerant picture was, however, to be shattered in the following year. Again, there was a dispute over the terms of the bond and the men struck. At Hetton, the owner began to evict strikers from collier cottages (as the bond permitted him to do) and replace them with blackleg labour, and in the ensuing melee a blackleg was murdered. Then, on Whit Monday, an unpopular and reactionary South Shields magistrate, Nicholas Fairles, was murdered by two colliers, one of whom got away. The other was hanged in chains on a gibbet at Jarrow Slake, near the murder scene, but colliers retrieved the body the same night and, it was thought, threw it in the river. Bitterness deepened. More blackleg labour was brought in from Wales, Staffordshire, Yorkshire and Wearside, the men by coach and their belongings by wagon. Cholera – the first of the great nineteenth-century epidemics to reach Europe – had now arrived in the area, but the evictions, even of sick families, continued. There was more violence, and troops came in to supervise the evictions and protect the blacklegs. The Welsh blacklegs had a particularly bad time, according to one account: 'Notwithstanding the deprecatory warnings of the pitmen, exhibited in the publication of a broadsheet list of accidents "by fire and flood", they descended the mines, but were found incompetent for the labours; and as their reception by the native colliers was more public than pleasing, and the danger of turbulence above ground as imminent as that of explosions of gas below, these immigrants, dreadfully thinned by the cholera, gradually retreated to their own districts.'

The strike faded out in August, but it left a bitter legacy which surfaced again in 1844, and 30,000 Durham miners again struck for better terms at the renewal of the bond. The leading coalowner was Lord Londonderry, who was unusual in being directly involved in working his coal rights rather than leasing them and merely collecting the royalties. He was also a leading member of the cartel which maintained the near-monopoly of supplying coal to London and keeping up the price. To the by now familiar features of strikes in the northeast – evictions, the importation of blacklegs, sporadic outbreaks of violence, Lord Londonderry added a new element when he issued a statement addressed to shopkeepers and tradesmen in Seaham, a town which he owned. This warned them that if they gave credit to strikers they would 'never have any custom or dealings with them from Lord Londonderry's large concerns that he can in any manner prevent'. Furthermore, he threatened to ruin Seaham by taking his trade to Newcastle. 'It is neither fair, just or equitable,' the statement went on, 'that the resident traders in his own town should combine and assist the infatuated workmen and pitmen in prolonging their own miseries by continuing an insane strike, and an unjust and senseless warfare against their proprietors and masters.' The strike, like its predecessors, failed, despite a pledge of support from the newly formed Miners' Association of Great Britain and Ireland, which itself had not long to live. A period of recession and enforced low wages in Northumberland followed as the boom in coal moved to the south Durham pits. Meanwhile, the lead in trade unionism moved towards the skilled artisan class, and it was to be three decades or more before it had any great impact on the lives of colliers. As for the bond, from 1844 onwards it slowly died away, though it continued in Durham until it was finally outlawed in 1872.

However, although it became a symbol of oppression – largely through the intransigence and sharp practice of employers – the bond did at least give the colliers of the northeast a nominal right to negotiate with the masters once a year, sometimes to their benefit but usually not, and it was the working practice closest to the annual wage round of today, for all that there have been attempts in some circles to represent annual bargaining as a modern aberration. There was less to be said, though, for a bastardized form of the bond system operated in Lancashire, which was less formal but made to work by placing colliers under a financial obligation. Men and lads old enough to handle a pick were hired for eleven months. The men then took a 'sub' of three or four pounds for themselves and a little less for their sons, agreeing to pay it off over the succeeding period. Sometimes the agreement would run for as long as it took to pay off the debt, which might be much longer than eleven months if earnings were low. It was the poorer and less provident colliers who were most vulnerable to this system, which was, however, localized and could fairly easily be avoided except by those really desperate for work.

By contrast, large areas of the country were screwed down in a system of labour organization which could almost have been designed to ferment bitterness, depress earnings, threaten safety and waste coal resources. This was the butty or charter-master system, whose heartland was the West Midlands but which was, as the capital cost of developing new pits increased, to spread through Staffordshire, Warwickshire and Shropshire on to Leicestershire, Derbyshire and Nottinghamshire until, in the 1860s, it was beginning to threaten even the deep-seated traditional practices of Yorkshire.

Butty worked like this. The butties or charter masters were, in effect, subcontractors, and there was a lot in common between butty and the subcontracting practices of the building trade in our own century; the fledgling trade unions objected to it for much the same reasons. It was a haven for 'cowboys'; it made sheer greed, without any other consideration, the prime mover of industry; and it was a mechanism by which each man exploited his neighbour for all he could get. (Notwithstanding this background, many butties were keen Methodists or Ranters.) The system as a whole was, in fact, made up of a chain of people, each of whom was dedicated to making the maximum profit, at whatever expense in human terms, out of the person below him. A landowner would let his mining rights to a coalmaster in return for a royalty based on the quality of the coal, often stipulating a minimum annual total payment. This at once lent a distinctive colour to the whole system, because it meant that only the best and easiest coal would be taken, while the minimum payment, though intended to prevent coalmasters from cornering the market by buying up 'futures' to be worked later, led to a certain amount of panic to reach each year's quota, especially if some unexpected misfortune such as flooding or a fall of rock delayed the hewers. This in turn produced instability in the demand for labour.

The coalmaster was responsible for sinking the shafts, building a furnace for ventilation and installing ventilation doors, if necessary, putting in pumping and winding equipment and driving the roadways between the pit bottom and the working face. All this involved considerable investment in advance of any revenue, but at this point the coalmaster's contribution to the enterprise, apart from providing labour for the pit top, was over; the attraction of butty for entrepreneurs was that it separated the cost of, as it were, building the factory from the cost of tooling it up for production. This was met by the butties, who contracted to deliver an agreed amount of coal to the pit bottom at an agreed price. The butties had to provide wagons, boys or, in the case of the thicker seams, horses for underground haulage, tools for the colliers and wages for preparatory work as well as for hewing and haulage once the working face was opened up.

The butty could start off with a small contract worked by, say, half a dozen men and a few boys, and gradually increase his business until he might employ thirty or more. The small man would hew alongside his men, setting the pace; as his business grew he would employ a foreman, called in the Midlands a 'doggy' and in Derbyshire a 'corporal', whose job was to ensure maximum production and, in particular, to keep the haulage running at top speed. The apprentices referred to in an earlier chapter were closely associated with the butty system. The butty's profit depended on the skill with which he could manipulate production, paid for by the ton, against the wages he paid out at day rates , and the work of apprentices played a vital part in this equation. Some butties took on ten or more, travelling to the workhouses of adjacent counties when the local supply dried up. An apprentice could not be bound until he was nine, but he could be taken on before that 'on trial'. From then on, he would work for his master until he was twenty-one, for his food and clothing and perhaps, if he had a soft-hearted butty, sixpence a week pocket money. It was ridiculous to defend apprenticeships – though some did – on the grounds that it took twelve years to learn the trade of using a pick. William Grove, a colliery manager in south Staffordshire who had been a butty, was more frank. Apprentices were, he said, 'essentially necessary for the success of the trade. We have such a call for boys in our workings, and if we had not got them bound to us, we should not have them under any sort of government, except from fortnight to fortnight. If we were to have boys and they had parents, they would change them from master to master, and encroach, and get twice as much for them as their labour is worth.' The system was a great relief: it relieved the workhouses of their burden, ratepayers of the poor rate, and butties of the necessity to pay decent wages.

It may be wondered how a butty could hold on to his apprentices when they became young men. The answer was that an apprentice who broke his indentures could be sent to jail, perhaps for a couple of months. This was the masterstroke of whoever it was first thought of applying the craft apprenticeship system to the pits: while there was no pretence that a pit apprenticeship led to any kind of craft status or expertise – who ever heard of a journeyman collier? – the apparatus of apprenticeship brought into play the sanctions of the law. As we saw earlier, workhouse apprentices who were too weak, or who became ill, or who were in any other way unsuitable for twelve years' hard labour, were simply taken back. Although it was technically an offence for a butty to break his side of the agreement, prosecutions that way round were unknown, and an apprentice could be turned out at a moment's notice if the butty thought fit. It was unlikely that a dismissed apprentice would go back to the workhouse voluntarily, becoming a charge on the poor rate, and that was all that mattered. So while a 20-year-old hewer, his own man, could earn about one pound a week in Staffordshire in the 1830s, an apprentice of the same age, doing the same work, earned his keep plus, with luck, sixpence. 'Whoever has been told of this apprenticeship of Staffordshire,' said one observer, 'has expressed indignation, and the same feeling which has knocked the chains off the African will soon bid the enslaved of Staffordshire go free.' This comment was made in 1841; slavery in the British Empire had been abolished eight years before.

Edward Oakley went down the pit in Wednesbury in 1810, when

he was eight, and received his first wages when he was twenty-one. At twelve he became a horse driver, for which he would have received, if he had not been an apprentice, about eight shillings a week. At fifteen he was hewing, and for the next six years worked for nothing at a job which would have earned a freeman four shillings a day. 'It was a hard time,' he said. 'The last part of it I thought very hard.' William Knighton of Denby, still working on the pit bank at seventy-four, looked back over fifty years to the days of his apprenticeship. It was, he said, 'sad, slavish work'.

The origins of the butty system are obscure. In its purest and most hated form, it was a nineteenth-century phenomenon. It may be significant that it almost exactly spanned the period during which Britain changed from a predominantly agricultural to a predominantly industrial economy; in its structure it had something in common with the gang system in agriculture, and with such occupations as hand nailmaking, the 'little maister' small workshop set-up in the Sheffield cutlery trade, and 'outwork' in the gloving and leathergoods trades. In the early days a man skilled at boring or sinking might, with a few mates or with members of his family, scrape together enough money to sustain them during the initial, non-productive stages of sinking a shaft or digging out a drift. There were examples of agreements under which landowners deferred rents or royalties until coal was actually produced, so that all that was needed to start with was a supply of primitive tools and some willing labour; though this could be laying up trouble for the future, since the need to pay off the debt could easily cripple a new enterprise. But sinking a shaft was, and is, a slow and expensive undertaking, and by the time the coal level had been reached capital would be exhausted. The subcontracting of the work of actually getting the coal out was a logical step. Though evidence is scarce and not easy to interpret, it seems that by the middle of the eighteenth century it was becoming common in the Midlands for a proprietor to sink the shaft and provide the underground roads, and then to let the right to get coal, which generally carried an obligation to deliver it to the pit bottom and sometimes to pay for it to be wound to the bank. There was a cooperative element in many of these early arrangements, but somewhere in the latter half of the century this was transmuted to the concept of the gang, in the charge of a gangmaster or butty. It is probable that the fever of canal-building which began with the Bridgewater Canal in 1761, and which, like railway-building in the next century, made use of a complex system of subcontracting and sub-subcontracting, stimulated similar developments in the pits, and there may be something in the fact that the butty system was most prominent in areas where the canal network was thickest.

The butty or charter master who won a contract had then to assemble a workforce of hewers and haulers and provide them with tools, candles and the means of haulage, though he might (and usually did) dock the cost of tools and candles from their earnings. The butty also had to provide timber for propping and shuttering, and it was a common complaint against the butties that they did not provide enough. Especially in the early weeks of opening up a new face, the butty could be financially on a knife-edge, and his men were balanced there with him; so it did not seem unreasonable for him to pay them a 'subsistence' (hence 'sub' for an advance of wages) and settle up in full when the coal was sold. (In fact, this practice was not confined to butty pits, but was also known in the larger enterprises of Scotland and North Wales.) Indeed, there was some merit in this method of payment, since it meant that the colliers could look forward to a sum of money with which they could, in theory at any rate, buy boots, clothes, blankets or a supply of meat for the winter; and meanwhile – again, in theory – it encouraged thrift. In practice, it worked out rather differently. From laying in a stock of candles and pickheads to sell to the men, it was but a short step to stocking basic food and drink to keep them going until reckoning day, and thus the link between butty and tommy was forged.

It was noticeable, as mining operations became increasingly mechanized from about 1800 onwards, that pits operated on the butty system tended to have the most primitive equipment. When winding by steam and the provision of rails for haulage underground were common, butty pits continued to wind by the horse gin and coal was still being dragged along underground on unrailed roads, often on unwheeled 'dans' or sledges. It was the butty pits, too, that employed most of the pit apprentices, who at the time of the 1851 census still numbered 30,000. Although butty was an early target for union action, it happened that Staffordshire, where the system was most deeply entrenched, lagged behind most other areas in union organization; as late as 1897 only about one fifth of Staffordshire colliers were union members. It was, as it turned out, technology and not union pressure that led to the steady fading out of butty. The system was not adaptable to an increasingly capital-intensive business, and the technological nature of mine-working towards the end of the nineteenth century called for qualified management and a responsible management structure. A court finding in 1867 that the owner and manager of a colliery, and not the butty, were ultimately responsible for safety was followed by a stipulation in the Coal Mines Act of 1872 that managers must be qualified and certified. This made butty, with its emphasis on a quick coal-getting job done as cheaply as possible, too much of a risk for management to bear, and by 1914 there were only a few pits, mainly in Staffordshire, where the system persisted. According to a correspondent who worked at Gresford Colliery near Wrexham in 1934, the leading man of a group of colliers was still known as the charter master at that time, but this seems to have been a survival of the term rather than of the system itself.

An ordinary collier just might – though it was unlikely because colliers were not savers by temperament – amass the £500 or so that it was reckoned, at the beginning of the nineteenth century, was needed by way of initial capital, and become a butty or charter master. A successful butty might just make enough money to become a coalmaster in a small way, in his own right. But most colliers were destined to spend their working lives at the point they had reached when, at the age of twenty or so, or sometimes younger, they first took to the pick. There were exceptions, though – just a few. The most notable and numerous of these were the 'free miners' of the Forest of Dean, a handful of whom are still their own masters of small workings.

The free miners received their status in return for the support given by Forest of Dean men to the Scottish campaign of Edward I. It is a hereditary right: to qualify you must be born of a free miner in the Hundred of St Briavels, a tract of land close to the Monmouthshire border, and must have worked in a mine for a year and a day. Originally, the value of the right (which carried a royalty to the Crown of one penny a ton) was in ironstone, but by the beginning of the eighteenth century coal was becoming more important. Each free miner was allowed up to three allotments – 'gales', they were called – of land beneath which to dig, and disputes in the operation of the system (the most common one being the breakthrough of one working into another) were settled by a special court which, however, tended to fade out of sight from time to time.

Until the eighteenth century, free miners had the right to cut timber from the forest for their own use in the pits, but somehow, perhaps because they abused the privilege – details of the matter are obscure – they lost it. Since many of the mines were drifts, reached by horizontal access which needed to be lined with timber, this was a serious blow, and records of eighteenth-century life in the Forest are full of complaints about what was, in effect, the poaching of trees, supposedly by free miners. One ruse, it was reported in 1735, was to bore 'large holes in trees that they may become dotard and decayed, and, as such, may be delivered to them gratis for the use of their collieries'. What was worse, 'some of the inferior officers of the Forest, finding offenders to go on with impunity, were not only grown negligent, but also connived at, if not partook in, the spoil daily committed'. The free miners had a particularly apt line in the naming of their pits, not being content, like big-time coalowners, with the name of the nearest village or a Christian name drawn from the family stock. Near Serridge there was, for example, the Stay and Drink pit; at Park End, the Hopewell; Go On and Prosper was opened in 1723, and the Rain Proof in 1744; near Yorkley there was the Long Looked For, and in 1757 the Now Found Out. The Littleworth near Ruerdean suggested no great hopes, and the Little Scare either a small fright or a good deal of optimism. Enthusiastic colliers might try for work at the Strip and At It pit, timid ones at the Never Fear, and those of classical bent at the Spero. Arthur's Folly was not encouraging, but there might be better luck at the Prosper, while there was always The Bold Defiance for those who liked a challenge. The Gentleman Colliers hinted at a decent way of earning a living, and The Pluck Penny at a cheeseparing one.

All this sounds very romantic and in the pioneering tradition, but the truth was rather different. The free miners were, almost literally, scratching a living; their enterprises were on a very small scale. In 1788, in one area of the Forest, seven pits employed only thirteen free miners, with eight boys and two women. Clearly there was no chance, at this level of activity, of accumulating enough capital to exploit the deeper seams, and as the easier coal was worked out the only solution was for the free miners to sell out their rights to companies with the capital to install steam engines, sink shafts, and lay down tramways. Although these rights were fast becoming useless to men without the means to make use of them, the Forest was a close and private place and there was a good deal of resentment at the takeover of historic rights by 'foreigners' such as Edward Protheroe, who owned four large collieries. This spilled over in 1831 in an outbreak of violence. It began with the sporadic breaking of plantation fences in the Forest, but quickly escalated into a full-scale attack on the Forest by some 200 men armed with axes and other implements. Special constables were hastily sworn in, but a defence force of about forty was all that could be mustered. On 8 June, the rioters 'began their work of destruction about seven o'clock, and we found it useless to attempt to stop them,' according to a Forest official. 'They were soon joined by others, and supplied with cider, and continued their work Wednesday, Thursday, Friday and Saturday, in which time they destroyed nearly one third of the fences in the Forest. . . . On Sunday military arrived, and they all dispersed.' The ringleader, Warren James, hid in a coal pit until he was persuaded to give himself up by a man with his eye on the reward offered, and James was subsequently sentenced to transportation for life.

A contemporary report concluded that this disturbance showed that 'an unsettled state of feeling existed in the minds of the foresters with regard to certain supposed rights', which was putting it mildly, and the free miners' rights were restated in an Act of 1838. But no Act of Parliament could alter the economic facts, which were that picking for coal in a twelve-yard radius, which was the size of a gale, was no longer a viable way of earning a living, and ruled out the possibility of using modern equipment, even if it could have been afforded. The selling or leasing of rights continued, and by 1874 it was reported that of 700 or 800 free miners on the books who were still alive, only about twenty were actually working their own pits, and there were few worthwhile gales left to grant. A Forest official told a House of Commons Select Committee in that year that in his view any hardship resulting from letting the system quietly fade out 'would be more sentimental than real. I do not think there would be any great hardship; but from my experience of the free miners, I think any proposal of that kind would be calculated to meet with considerable opposition.' On the whole, though, it hardly seemed worthwhile to interfere with ancient customs, and indeed the free miners' own small pits remained outside the scope of nationalization in 1947. In 1951, it was reckoned that there were between thirty and forty of them.

The free miners of the Forest of Dean were not the only ones to cherish the idea of self-employment, though they were almost the only ones to succeed, in however small a way, for any length of time. The success of the cooperative movement from the mid-nineteenth century inspired miners' organizations to extend the principle to their own industry. There were two attempts in the 1870s – encouraged by a short-lived boom in coal profits – to establish cooperative pits with union funds, both in Derbyshire. In 1873, with heavy investment from the Durham Miners' Association as well as from individual miners, some of whom were to lose all their savings, a company was formed to buy the rundown Monkswood pit near Chesterfield. But the workings had been overvalued, and the new company had badly underestimated the amount of investment needed to make it profitable; in the first year there was a loss of nearly £11,000, over a quarter of the paid-up capital, and the experiment ended sadly with the cooperators declaring that they had been swindled and suing unsuccessfully for their money back. At Shirland, some ten miles to the south, the South Yorkshire Miners' Association went into a similar venture, though relying in their case on outside capital. This ended with a loss of £31,000, largely, it seems, because collieries could not be run by committees of management.

From time to time there have been other attempts, on a smaller scale, to establish cooperatives in the pits. There were, for example, a number of sporadic attempts in the Somerset coalfield in the 1920s. There were talks about a cooperative takeover at Clutton, south of Bristol, when a worked-out pit, whose production was said to be not enough to keep its own boilers in steam, was closed by the owners in 1921, but they came to nothing. This was, of course, the year of the great coal strike, and a group of workers opened a drift mine in the same area which, however, lasted for only two years or so. In 1923, there was another attempt to establish a cooperative pit near Clutton – a more ambitious proposal this time, involving £17,000 capital which could not, in the event, be raised. The longest lasting of the Somerset cooperatives was at Farrington Gurney, near Midsomer Norton, which survived from 1921 into postwar nationalization. It began when Farrington Colliery was closed as a result of the 1921 strike. About twenty men formed a cooperative to sink a drift which had to be abandoned two years later because of the threat of flooding from old workings; but another attempt was made nearby, this time with success. It was a condition of employment that all men over eighteen had to be shareholders, and the enterprise – which in 1926 was producing only eight or nine tons of coal a day – was a curious mixture of Victorian and modern liberal conditions. Coal was hauled out with the guss and crook, drawing a putt, a wooden sledge containing up to two hundredweight of coal. This practice continued until the Coal Board took over in 1947. Yet, on the other hand, it was the first pit in Somerset to introduce holidays with pay. In 1941, employing forty-three men and boys, the cooperative was producing a hopelessly uneconomic 130 tons a week, and six years later it was nationalized for compensation of about £9500, closing down in 1949.

What had already started to happen by that time was an extension of the process begun when the first coalmaster replaced his horse gin with a winding engine: the stealthy takeover of the pits by mechanization. As long as steam was the only form of motive power available, this process was of course confined to the surface, but as early as the 1860s there were coal cutters in use in Durham, operated by compressed air. These were later joined by electrically operated cutters, but the introduction of both types was slow, mainly because only the newer pits could accommodate them but also because of growing worries over the rivalry of oil as the fuel of the twentieth century. By 1925, still only a third of Britain's collieries had cutters. This pattern was echoed in mechanical haulage underground. But today, with the old pits weeded out and closed, and with greater confidence in coal as a result of the huge rise in oil prices in the 1970s, virtually all Britain's coal is mechanically cut and hauled. The effect on production statistics has been dramatic. In 1913, British miners were producing 233 tons of coal each per year; in 1980–81 this had risen to 562 tons. At the same time, there had been a drastic reduction in the workforce; for every hundred men at work in the pits in 1913, there were by 1981 only eighteen. In 200 years miners had moved from sheer backbreaking physical toil in conditions of near (and in Scotland, actual) slavery to the status of technicians and engineers. However, the changes were dictated by economics, and not by humanitarianism, legislation, or even unionism.

In 1841, Isabel Hogg, coal bearer at Penston Colliery in East Lothian, looked back from her fifty-three years of life of misery. She married at sixteen to give her man her labour; had four daughters, all bearers, but one permanently laid up after a miscarriage; became the breadwinner at thirty-three when her husband had to stop work because of short breath; and was a widow at forty-four. 'You must just tell the Queen Victoria,' she said, 'that we are good loyal subjects; women people here don't mind work, but they object to horsework; and that she would have the blessings of all the Scotch coalwomen if she would get them out of the pits, and send them to other labour.' But Queen Victoria could have done nothing; King Coal listens only to Mammon.

7

'STRONG FEELINGS OF MUTUAL ATTACHMENT'

Only passing mention has been made so far of union activity in the coalfields. This may seem surprising. National miners' strikes, with those of railwaymen and dockers, dominated industrial relations in the years immediately before the First World War, greatly to the alarm, as Harold Nicolson wrote, of those statesmen and citizens who saw in them 'the presage of a rising of the proletariat and the injection into our political life of the dangerous Continental theory of syndicalism, with its battle cry of "they who rule industrially will rule politically" and its firm belief in the efficacy of direct action.' Similar forebodings were felt again in the 1920s. Since the strikes of the early 1970s, miners' union leaders have confirmed their place in the demonology of middle Britain, and even the hint of a miners' strike can still win acres of press space. Yet against all this, the record of the miners' unions in *national* terms – in terms of the industry itself, things are rather different – is a mixed one. Two bloody and bitter years between 1910 and 1912, which included the virtual military occupation of the Rhondda and Aberdare valleys in what was the most serious confrontation of its kind in three centuries, resulted in the colliers' achievement of a minimum wage agreement – but this was to prove in the 1920s and 1930s a hollow victory. The strikes of the 1920s, culminating in the General Strike of 1926, ended in debilitation, defeat, and political desperation – so much so that, for example, the miners' leader Arthur Cook, coiner of the slogan 'Not a penny off the pay, not a minute on the day', consorted after 1926 with Sir Oswald Mosley, who was attempting to achieve power through the Independent Labour Party and who was to be a regular speaker for some years at the Durham Miners' Gala. It will be seen in the next chapter how low, by the mid-1930s, had sunk the unions' ability to look after the basic protection of its members. And when the nationalization of the pits came in 1947 it was through a government in whose election not the miners – who had been exempted from military service – but members of the armed forces had the decisive voice. Nor, once the initial euphoria was over, did nationalization turn out to lead colliers into the promised land. They found the accountants of the National Coal Board no less hard-faced than those of capitalist managements.

On the national scene, miners have always been vulnerable in two respects: demagoguery has held a fatal fascination for them, and they have lacked the ability to see when they were being made use of. An early leader, for example, was Alexander Macdonald, a self-educated Scottish collier described by Beatrice and Sydney Webb as having 'a florid style and somewhat flashy personality'. Later there was Arthur Cook, 'an inspired idiot drunk with his own words, dominated by his own slogans'. However, perhaps the views of the Webbs and their patronizing Fabian circle should be treated with caution; in her diary Beatrice dismissed the miners of Derbyshire as 'a stupid, stolid lot of men characterized by fairmindedness and kindliness', qualities unlikely to appeal to such a bleak architect of bureaucracy as Mrs Webb. What is certain, however, is that a large number of those who achieved political importance through their early work in miners' organizations, Nye Bevan among them, made their way as soon as possible towards orchards where the fruits were sweeter.

At local level and within the industry, however, the picture was different, and increasingly from the second half of the nineteenth century onwards union pressure was inching forward in such areas as fair weighing, safety and welfare. The pity is that miners came to recognize their potential political muscle some fifty years after it had gone into decline; if the strength of the 1970s had been available from a workforce four times larger before 1914, the whole course of British political history, perhaps even of the First World War itself, might have been changed.

Early trade-union activity in the coalfields emerges from several patches of mist. One was the Nonconformist tradition, and reactionaries like Lord Sidmouth may well have wondered, as his lordship did in 1812, how easily a Methodist bible-class meeting might turn into something more seditious. Another was the

Friendly Society movement, and it has been noted in an earlier chapter that many coalmasters were keen to keep their eyes closely on such societies, even to the extent of virtually taking them over. Another was the tendency of the working class to riot and randy, especially when they had just been paid, and it would be difficult, from contemporary accounts, to distinguish the riots of the eighteenth and early nineteenth centuries from more legitimate trade-union protests – especially since the magistracy often took no trouble to make a distinction and arranged for the Riot Act to be read regardless. The riotous activities of the colliers of Kingswood near Bristol have already been mentioned, and in most parts colliers joined with a will in any protest that might be going against the price of corn or a change in the calendar. Towards the end of the eighteenth century, however, the typical miners' protest began increasingly to take the form of a strike rather than a bread riot, and to have as its target the employer rather than local tradesmen. These strikes were usually confined to one pit or one locality, and in as much as they were organized at all in any modern sense, the organization rarely survived the one event. An account of a strike in Northumberland in 1811 lends to the proceedings quite a homely touch. 'As the colliers form a distinct body of men, and seldom associate with others,' it says, 'they entertain strong feelings of mutual attachment. When they combine or *stick* for the purpose of raising their wages, they are said to spit upon a stone together, by way of cementing their confederacy. This appears to be a very old custom, the origin of which is lost in the remoteness of time.' It is true that spitting to strike a bargain is an ancient custom, still to be seen in use at, for example, horse fairs, but, given the period when this passage was written, it is more likely that spitting on a stone was a substitute for anything more overt, which might have involved prosecution under the Combination Acts.

These were introduced, trade by trade, in 1799 and 1800. Under them, workmen who combined to bring about an increase in wages or a reduction in working hours could be brought before a magistrate and, on conviction, be sentenced to three months in the county jail or two months' hard labour. The Acts were vicious in conception, excluding even the membership of friendly societies and funeral clubs, and they were as viciously operated. There was, for example, in existence an Act prohibiting the payment of wages in the iron industry in truck or tommy, and this applied not only to the ironworks themselves but also to the collieries associated, as many were, with them. Truck was, however, too profitable a system to be cast away lightly by employers, and it also enabled them to conceal wage cuts by raising tommy-shop prices. But any combined action aimed at the enforcement of one law, the Truck Act, fell foul of the Combination Acts, and since the operation of the latter was in the hands of magistrates the protection of the Truck Act effectively disappeared. The Combination Acts scotched for a generation the chance of effective trade-union organization, and until they were repealed in 1824 and 1825 the protests and frustrations of colliers and others continued to be expressed, not in the orderly meetings that might have sprung from the example of friendly society and bible class, but in occasional riots and their inevitable clashes between rioters and yeomanry. The most celebrated of these was at St Peter's Fields, Manchester (Peterloo) in 1819, and resulted in the deaths of eleven people, including two women and a child, and over 400 wounded; but there were many more isolated, less serious and less well-reported incidents during the years of the Combination Acts. At Bilston in Staffordshire in 1821, for example, a collier was killed when troops intervened in a fracas between miners and blacklegs. The wonder is that there were not many more. In the wake of the French Revolution it had become government policy to distribute troops widely across the country, especially near manufacturing towns. 'Troops were distributed,' according to J.L. and Barbara Hammond, 'all over the country, and the North and Midlands and the manufacturing region in the southwest came to resemble a country under military occupation. The officers commanding in the different districts reported on the temper and circumstances of their districts just as if they were in a hostile or lately conquered country; soldiers were moved about in accordance with fluctuations in wages or employment, and the daily life of the large towns was watched anxiously and suspiciously by magistrates and generals.' The armed forces' distance from the people over whom they kept watch had been ensured by a huge programme of barrack-building, replacing the earlier custom of stationing troops in ale houses. By 1815, the Hammonds say, there were 155 such barracks capable of holding 17,000 cavalry and 138,000 infantry, a sizeable force to hold down a population of some thirteen million. It was an extension to England of the system by which it had been hoped (and the hope proved false) to subdue the Highlands of Scotland after 1715.

When the Combination Acts were dismantled, this formidable army of occupation was not, and it played a full part in the events of the next few decades as the trade unions began to assert themselves. Among those quick to take advantage of the repeal of the Acts were the colliers of Tyneside, who in 1825 and 1826 published pamphlets describing conditions in their pits, which led to the formation of the short-lived Association of Colliers on the Rivers Tyne and Wear. The activities of the Association have been described in chapter 6. Over the next two decades, there were similar sporadic efforts in the northeast and elsewhere, but they tended to fizzle out once the particular cause round which they had been formed had been won or – as was more usual – lost. Scotland's first union, for example, was founded in 1835, but was disbanded two years later after a courageous but defeated strike lasting four months. The first hint that it might be possible to establish a permanent movement with wider political objectives came with the activities of the Chartists in 1839.

Being for the most part skilled artisans, the Chartists were socially at some distance from colliers, though they had links through Nonconformism. Once they began to organize for action, however, the various strands of the movement began to fall apart, Cheshire men talking, for example, of obtaining civil rights 'by the bullet, the pike and the bayonet', while Leicester men wanted peaceful protest. Organizers of political movements had as yet learned nothing of the art and science of fieldwork, and so it was that the 1839 Chartist rising tended to take on local colouring, and so dissipate its effect, rather than to remain cohesive and national. In South Wales, for example, it locked itself into the local battle with coal- and ironmasters over truck which had been going on for twenty years. In a riot in 1831, the colliers of Merthyr Tydfil had wrecked the debtors' court where the records of their truck accounts were kept, and troops had come in to restore order. There were widespread sackings, and blackleg labour came in. A secret organization, the 'Scotch Cattle', was set up to counter the blacklegs and the truck shops, and there was a campaign of violence and arson. In South Wales, it was these men that the Chartist movement took on board – to the horror, no doubt, of the gentle stocking weavers of Leicester. The involvement of the Scotch

Cattle led to the celebrated attack on Newport which ended in panicky official orders to fire, the death of a dozen or more Chartists and the flight in confusion of the rest. In Northumberland and Durham, enthusiasm for the Chartists centred round the concept of the 'sacred month' for which, it was supposed, men would strike and at the end of which the demands of the Charter would be granted by a defeated and abashed establishment.

It is too easy to look back on these events with the superior wisdom of the late twentieth century. The Chartist organizers had to set local action in the context of national issues, and to engage the support of men most of whom were, on their own admission, illiterate and had little idea where London was, let alone what Westminster signified. To the mass of the Chartist audience, Parliament was a concept which there was great difficulty in grasping except in terms of slogans; and indeed, it is not easy to see, in the terms of the time, how a vote for a man to go to Westminster, wherever that was, could help bring about an improvement in wages or conditions at Felling, Tyne Main, Hetton or in the Rhondda. No doubt the outbreaks of violence, often mindless violence, which attended the 1839 strike in the northeast were an expression of the frustrations felt by men who could only listen to words, but who daily felt the realities of the docked wage, the fine, the threat of dismissal and eviction and the refusal of credit. The relatively sophisticated leaders of the 1839 Charter knew perfectly well that what they were engaged in was only a political gesture, but in order to make it effective they had to persuade the signatories that the sacred month really would last until universal suffrage and the other demands had been met. In 1839 the colliers heard for the first time the lesson that was to be repeated time and time again over the next century: *to be promised* is not the same as *to have delivered*. Faced with the almighty power of a Lord Londonderry or a Lord Durham, who really must have seemed to the inhabitants of their colliery villages like the unknown guests at every meal and the unknown listeners to every conversation, the simplistic politics of Sunday-school educated pitmen's leaders had no chance. Indeed, so outgunned were the colliers that managers and owners could afford to be magnanimous. Despite the many threats that, in the words of Lord Londonderry, 'pitmen who hold off work, and continue in the union ... will be marked by his agents and overmen, and will never be employed in his collieries again,' there does not seem to have been widespread victimization after the outbursts of 1839. Looking back on the year, for example, William Hunter, viewer (manager) of Walbottle Colliery near Newcastle, seemed inclined to let bygones be bygones: 'The sacred month was begun here,' he said, 'but the magistrates were very active, and were assisted by the military. Four men were imprisoned for refusing to work, and fined, the others who rebelled, being a large portion of the whole, heavily. These measures restored order, and since that period the same persons have conducted themselves in an exemplary manner.' The reason why it was still possible to prosecute the strikers was that, under the legislation that followed the repeal of the Combination Acts, striking was lawful only over wages and hours, and the sacred month was, of course, a political strike.

What the Charter of 1839 had certainly shown was that magistracy and military, between them, were still in control, and such trade-union activity as there was began to turn from direct action to the slow improvement of conditions by less threatening means. In Staffordshire, a temporarily strong local union exacted some useful concessions on conditions in the 1840s, though the trade depression of the late 1840s robbed it of most of its gains and it broke up in 1849, creating a mood of disenchantment which endured in that area until the present century; as late as 1913, fewer than one third of Staffordshire miners were in the union. The same trade decline of the 1840s did for a hopeful development in the North of England, where the Miners' Association of Great Britain and Ireland had, by 1844, attracted – or so it claimed – a membership of 100,000. Three years later, in the face of the depression, it collapsed. Attempts in 1850 to revive it failed, and as wages continued to spiral downwards, taking with them the aspirations of the colliers for improved conditions, so did union membership. Both wages and union membership reached their lowest point in 1855–56.

The fortunes of the coal trade were a reflection of the wider changes that were taking place in British society in mid-century. Britain was about to become Great Britain, and finished products, not raw materials like coal, were going to effect the transformation. The Great Exhibition of 1851, its Crystal Palace packed with a million artefacts, was an indication of the way things were going; and the interest of those who hoped to ride to political power on the back of trade unionism had passed back to the skilled artisan class: the toolmakers, the engineers, the pattern-makers. Chartism was dead after its 1848 debacle – the seven million signatures had turned out to be about three million, many of which were such as 'Queen Victoria', 'The Duke of Wellington', 'Old Nick', 'Captain Swing', 'Ned Ludd' and so on – and the threat of revolution had faded decently into the past. The Irish famines of the 1840s had brought to the mainland labour market many thousands of willing men. The export trade in coal was faltering because too much British mining expertise had been exported to Germany and Belgium and America. The first pressures of free trade were beginning to be felt among farmers. At the end of 1848, the bursting of the Railway Mania bubble signalled the end of the first Railway Age.

Nevertheless, these were not entirely empty years for organized labour in the pits. In 1850, the principle of government inspection of mines had been established, though the instrument for doing so was (and remained for nearly a century) pitifully inadequate. Perhaps because union activity seemed dead or otherwise safe, the Friendly Societies Act of 1855 gave unions legal status. And in 1856, the 'florid and flashy' Alexander Macdonald came roaring down from Glasgow to Yorkshire with a programme of action consisting mainly of items which had nothing to do with rates of pay. He sought, to quote his own words, 'A better Mines Act, true weighing, the education of the young, the restriction of the age till twelve years, the reduction of the working hours to eight in every twenty-four, the training of managers, the payment of wages weekly in the current coin of the realm, no truck, and many other useful things too numerous to mention.' Macdonald was lucky, or perhaps well informed, in the choice of Yorkshire as his platform. Within two years the South Yorkshire owners had embarked on a lockout, which led to the formation of a determined district association of colliers. Coalfield confrontation was now moving out of the phase in which it was customary for the troops to be called out to face strikers (though it was later to move into it again), and in 1859 Parliament passed an Act expressly permitting 'peaceful persuasion' in the cause of wages and working hours, a landmark still in trade-union history.

The issue of 'true weighing' was a long-standing and contentious one. Tubs of coal were marked with a tally stick, or chalked with the collier's number, and credited to the individual collier's account. If they were underweight, or contained stone, the appropriate amount was docked or a fine was imposed. No doubt some were underweight, or a collier would occasionally try his luck by putting in a bit of stone, but the fact that the decision on payment was made on the say-so of an owner's man was a running sore of suspicion and resentment. For the first time, the Mines Regulation Act of 1860 gave colliers the right to appoint their own checkweighmen, though there was still another battle to be fought over the checkweighmen's right to test the weighing machines. The Act was psychologically important, though, since this was the first acknowledgement of any colliers' rights on the management side of the pit.

Alexander Macdonald's programme, with additions, formed the agenda of a national conference called in Leeds in 1863 with the object of forming a national miners' union. It was here that it became evident that, although linked by their common product, not all colliers thought alike; a serious rift emerged between the Northumberland and Durham miners and the rest. The issue was the difference between the working pattern of the hewers or getters and those of the haulage boys. The hewers worked an eight-hour day, but the boys, since they had to clear all the coal won up to the end of the hewers' shift, worked for longer. It was proposed to reduce the boys' hours to eight, in line with the men, and where men and boys were working alongside, shift by shift, this presented no great problem: the boys could arrive late, by which time coal for them to haul would have accumulated, and they could stay on after the men to clear up. But in Northumberland and Durham the hewers worked in two shifts, with one shift of boys to haul for both. The organization formed at Leeds, the Miners' National Association, was, like all miners' unions, made up of men who had 'got their number' as hewers, and so the interests of the boys were not particularly well represented. Even if they had been, the result might have been no different, because although the argument rested on the possibility of the effect of a change in working practice on the hewers' wages, the real issue was the change itself. When, even today, miners come out over some apparently trifling management decision, they are not necessarily being bloody-minded but simply expressing their arch-conservatism. However, the result was that the miners of the northeastern coalfield went

their own way, and stayed there until the passing of the Eight Hours
Act of 1909. They had, in any case, their own particular cause,
which was the abolition of the yearly bond. This was finally
achieved in 1872, though in practice it was by that time a rarity.
Meanwhile, the newly found harmony of Leeds, even discounting
the pitmen of the northeast, soon disintegrated. The Association
was thought to be too Yorkshire-biased, and in 1869 Lancashire
and Cheshire men set up their own organization, the Amalgamated
Association of Miners, which spread down through Wales in the
next few years. The process of division and subdivision began to be
reminiscent of the constantly changing scene of Nonconformist
schism. When it came down to it, local conditions were of greater
significance to miners than national causes or humanitarian
principles; it proved impossible to interest men from areas where
the butty system was not a problem in the fight of their colleagues in
areas where it still was, and the men of the northeast saw nothing
wrong in their haulage boys working eleven hours or more to bridge
two shifts if, by doing so, the price of Durham coal was thereby kept
down and the demand up. In any case, half-marrers became
full-marrers, and in due time got their collier's number, and their
eight-hour shift. And so union activity began to break down into a
ragtag and bobtail of organizations, the Durham Miners' Mutual
Confident, the Ayrshire Miners' Federal, and all the rest, shifting,
federating, splitting, re-forming over the twenty years or so to
1888.

The individual colliery branch was called the Lodge, a relic of
the friendly societies which had in turn looked for inspiration to
Freemasonry. That one of the unions' other ancestral links, with
the chapels, persisted well into living memory is indicated by a story
told by a Glamorgan man, John Williams, to George Ewart Evans.
John Williams's father was chairman of the Lodge as well as
secretary of the chapel, and on one occasion he led a deputation
from the Lodge to see the owner and his manager about a dispute
involving a halfpenny a ton. They started with a prayer, 'asking the
blessing of God now on the meeting'. It came to deadlock, and
'they'd all stand up and pray again for God's guidance'. And God
was evidently listening, because although the meeting broke up
without agreement an accommodation was later reached. This
piece of negotiation, ludicrous by current standards, must have
taken place about the turn of this century.

Towards the end of the nineteenth century, however, times were too serious for miners' leaders to rely, on the one hand, on the power of prayer or, on the other, to indulge in the luxury of schism. The district unions encouraged, if nothing else, colliers in one pit to compare their lot with those in a neighbouring one, and the result was often a skirmish. At South Medomsley, County Durham, there was a strike, typical of hundreds during these years, in 1885. The South Medomsley men had discovered that their pay was 10 per cent less than the county average. The management proposed to make a further cut, and the men struck, only to find the strike broken when, under police guard, blacklegs came in from Consett and Newcastle. Seven years later the entire combine of Durham coalowners demanded a 10 per cent cut in wages, and locked the men out when they rejected the scheme. After two months, with their supply of pit coal used up and their families approaching desperation, the men gave in, only to be told that the owners' demand had now gone up to 13½ per cent. After more weeks of misery, 10 per cent was agreed. Although, during this period, the price of coal was fluctuating, the hard economic facts only went to show just how much money the owners had been making. South Medomsley Colliery, for example, changed hands in 1862 for £7000. Ten years later it was sold again – for £70,000 and an annual rent of £2000.

The outcome of the industrial skirmishes of the 1880s and 1890s was the emergence of the Miners' Federation of Great Britain, founded in Manchester in 1888. Before long, the only sizeable body of miners remaining outside the Federation were those of the northeast, whose policy on hours of work kept them aloof until, after the Eight Hours Act of 1909, they too came into the Federation. In the 1890s, the price of coal continued to fall in the face of foreign competition for export markets, and there was a call for a 25 per cent cut in wages – the cue for the first demonstration by the Federation that the colliers' industrial muscle could be put to work nationally. In 1893, 300,000 men in Yorkshire, Lancashire and the Midlands were out for five months, and a further 100,000 in South Wales and Scotland for a shorter period.

At this point, the history of miners' unions begins to shade off imperceptibly into the history of the Labour movement and the Labour Party, themes which are outside the scope of this book. The minimum wage won by the bloody struggle of 1912 became, as is the way with such things, a maximum wage as well, once the demands of the 1914–18 War were over. In their four reports of 1919, the majority of the members of the government-appointed Sankey Commission had harsh words to say about the coalowners' stewardship of the industry; for example (Interim Report, 20 March 1919): 'The present system of ownership and working in the coal industry stands condemned, and some other system must be substituted for it.' Three months later the chairman, Sir John Sankey, and six of the Commission's thirteen members were prepared to spell out what the substitute might be: 'That Parliament be invited immediately to pass legislation acquiring the Coal Royalties for the State and paying fair and just compensation to the owners.' The industry had, in fact, been government controlled during the war, and the government's response to the Sankey Commission's report was that, so far from taking up the majority proposal for nationalization, control was to be abolished. The result was the 1921 strike, which began on 1 April and, after the Black Friday of 15 April when the railwaymen and transport workers went back on their 'Triple Alliance' agreement and called off the General Strike, dragged on until, at the end of June, the miners had to go back on the owners' terms. Under cover of this defeat for the miners, the owners exacted their revenge. Even lower wages and longer hours were to be the order of the day. In Somerset, the owner of Farrington Colliery, who had given a 'back to work – or else' warning during the strike, was as good as his word and shut the place down. At a neighbouring pit, Clutton, the men had defied the union and stayed at work for less than the minimum wage. A closure notice was issued, all the same. Then we'll work on any terms, said the men, just to keep our jobs. Enough is enough, said the Somerset Miners' Association, and so the pit closed.

The Sankey Commission report had been profoundly disturbing, despite the dissension of almost half its members, and it was thought advisable to have something less inflammatory on paper. Accordingly, a Royal Commission was appointed under Sir Herbert Samuel. Samuel managed to produce a report to which all his fellow commissioners could consent, but which managed to upset everyone, owners as well as miners. It proposed a temporary cut in wages, or alternatively an extension of hours for the same pay; and at the same time the state purchase of coal reserves. The report appeared on 11 March 1926, and by 1 May the coalfields were silent. The abject story of the General Strike is well covered elsewhere and need not be repeated here. After fourteen days the miners found themselves beleaguered again, and six months later they surrendered. In the next chapter 250 or so victims of that debacle are discussed, but there were many others: the 250,000 who uprooted themselves from South Wales over the next few years and went to find work in Oxford and Swindon, Coventry and Dagenham; the men of Clandown (once the giant of the Somerset coalfield) and Priston, Middle Pit, Newbury and Moorewood, all near Radstock; and the thousands who simply rotted in their houses as, stick by stick, their furniture was sold and their watches were pawned and they came, at last, to be sufficiently reduced to qualify for national succour.

There are two footnotes to be added to this chapter, neither concerned with mainstream miners' union activity – in the political sense, anyway – but both, perhaps, shedding some light on it. In 1871, there was held in Durham a meeting which was to become enshrined in Labour-movement history: the Durham Big Meeting or, as it is more usually known, the Durham Miners' Gala. It was, and is, principally a drinking spree, a mid-July picnic – Durham's answer to the Northumberland miners, who actually call their equivalent celebration the Northumberland Miners' Picnic – and although shop windows are boarded up the pubs keep their doors open. The Big Meeting must have been something in 1911, when there were 152,000 miners in Durham. It was still something in 1925, when the Bishop of Durham had been incautious enough, the Sunday before, to preach in the cathedral a sermon attacking the miners. According to legend, he was seen treading the racecourse turf on the day of the Gala and pitched into the river, and a police launch had to rescue him. The truth, it seems, is minimally less exciting: the colliers had seen a man of the cloth, an innocent dean, and taken it out on him.

Down the years the Big Meeting has attracted (indeed, its organizers have been beseeched by) the big guns of the Labour movement, which in more recent years has tended to mean the Labour Party. The freethinking Annie Besant and Charles Bradlaugh spoke there in the days when they thought there might be something in it for them; Sir Oswald Mosley, also finding a platform and trying to make it work for him; Arthur Cook, who would speak anywhere; Nye Bevan; Tony Benn and Lord

Stansgate, together on the same bill; Michael Foot, who in 1983 held the record for the number of appearances; Neil Kinnock. They have all looked down from the balcony of the Royal County Hotel (A A four star, 122 rooms with showers; 'stylishly modernized', says Egon Ronay) on the waving banners, many remembering pits that are no longer open, for the 152,000 miners of 1911 are now shrunk to less than 20,000, and falling. The typical pit banner has a central figure surrounded by lesser lights. Wardley had Lenin in the centre, flanked by, among others, James Connolly of the Irish Citizens' Army and George Harvey, the Wardley Lodge secretary in the 1920s. Banners can be repainted; does there lurk in the heart of one of them, one wonders, the hysterical, absurd face of Sir Oswald Mosley, hastily blanked out in favour of some Lodge official? The occasion is an incitement to fantasy, a glorious piece of high hokum. 'When this Gala is over,' said Neil Kinnock in 1983 – he was then only one of many candidates for the Labour leadership – 'we should go among the people of England, communicate with them, speak to them, listen to them and find out what they have to say.' In Wales, they call this *hwll*; in Durham, they may well call it something else. But the Gala is to Labour politicians what the Windmill Theatre used to be to stand-up comics: a necessary date on the way to the top. And the speeches are just about as irrelevant to the real business of the Big Meeting, which is drinking, as the comedians were to the real business of the Windmill, which was *tableaux vivants*. That is why politicians can get away in Durham with empty rhetoric which would get them hooted off the platform at any serious political gathering.

It is a long way from the Royal County Hotel, Durham, to the village of Dunkerton in Somerset, the scene for my second footnote. Dunkerton is about halfway between Radstock and Bath on the A367. The road drops sharply into the Cam Valley, crosses the river, and climbs out as steeply past Severcombe Farm. A railway used to run through the valley, much used as a film location because of its apparent rural isolation. But – as happens so often on the Somerset coalfield – tucked away, on the left as you go towards Bath, are the remains of what was at one time Somerset's largest pit. They sank the shafts at Dunkerton in 1903. The first coal came up in 1906, and by 1912 there were 700 men at work, producing 3000 tons of coal a week. It was an operation more in tune with the eighteenth century than with the twentieth; in the interests of productivity, only the easily accessible coal was taken, with the result that the pit was worked out within less than twenty years. Corners were cut in other ways, too, including safety and, of course, wages. Even the historians of the rundown Somerset coalfield, who on the whole tend to be undisturbed by the symptoms of rampant capitalism evident in the area in pre-nationalization days, give a black mark to Dunkerton.

There came about in 1909 a dispute at Dunkerton which owed nothing to the miners' unions but which seems to have sprung from the exploitation of people who, driven to the extreme, acted for themselves. It has been mentioned earlier that haulage boys did not figure in union activities, since they were held to be dependent on the hewers and subject to them. (A Glamorgan collier told George Ewart Evans: 'If a boy even ventured an opinion in amongst the men, it was the biggest crime you could commit. . . . The boys never fraternized with the men; they were always kept strictly in their place.') Haulage lads in Somerset were known as 'carting boys', though some of them were in their early twenties. The life of a carting boy at Dunkerton was rough. You took the guss and crook – the belt and chain of pre-Victorian coalfields which were a distant memory almost everywhere else – and hitched it to a putt, as they called it in Somerset, and hauled this putt – which had runners, not wheels – over ill-made roads for perhaps threepence (just over 1p) per ton. The carting boys at Dunkerton asked in 1907 for something like fivepence (2p) per ton. Eighteen months later, their claim having got nowhere, they struck.

The carting boys of Dunkerton had hit upon something that haulage lads everywhere should have thought of: if the coal cannot be brought out, a pit is paralysed. The strike went on. A few miners continued to go below, to such protests that mounted police had to be brought in. Then, on 22 January 1909, when the strike was three months old, the 'Dunkerton outrage' took place.

It was not a very big outrage, even by the modest standards of British labour history. Its significance was that it occurred in an unlikely quarter of the country, in a workforce which had a relatively quiet history, and among a sector of that workforce which had not hitherto (nor has since) made such an outburst of spontaneous feeling. The facts are hazy, but it seems that on that Friday the colliery surveyor, Edgar Heal, who happened to be the manager's son, received a complaint from two men who were not on strike that they had been threatened as they went on shift. He told them not to worry, but to carry on as usual. Armed with this authority, the two men went to work, and, faced with what looked like open provocation, the strikers, some 200 strong, organized a protest march to the home of the colliery manager. It was dark by the time they arrived – they had been delayed by the urge to break some windows on the way – and the manager was not at home. His son Edgar, however, was; and he evidently panicked at the sight of the approaching men who, whether their mood was ugly or merely noisy, looked frightening. Edgar Heal went to the door and fired two revolver shots into the air. The crowd began to stone the Heals' house, and Edgar went inside and returned with a loaded shotgun. This time he fired into the crowd, three or maybe four times.

At this point, with about a dozen men and boys lying injured, the police arrived and Edgar Heal vanished, to be arrested in Bristol the next day. By that time, twenty-one strikers had also been arrested, some for further offences of assault and riot on the Saturday.

The outcome of the case, which came up a month later, was instructive for those who believed in the impartiality of the law. Edgar Heal, charged with unlawful and malicious wounding, was acquitted. Ten of the strikers were sent down to hard labour, and another five given more lenient sentences. You could, in 1909, if you were a member of the employing classes, push your luck to the limit and get away with it. If you were one of the employed, and tried to push your luck even half as far, you could end up doing hard labour. The strike, incidentally, ended in the same week as the court case. The boys and their masters split the difference.

8

THE NIGHT GRESFORD
BLEW UP

In the second half of the nineteenth century and in the first decades of our own, there were countless Acts of Parliament designed to regulate working conditions, prevent accidents and control employment in the pits. Almost every one demonstrated the inefficacy of those that had gone before and the ability of owners to get round, or simply ignore, the restrictions of legislation. The Act of 1842 prohibited the employment underground of women and girls, and of boys under ten, and the employment of persons under fifteen as winding enginemen. As noted earlier, this was widely ignored; there were still women at work underground in South Wales in 1851, and according to George Orwell, who in 1936 heard of a Lancashire woman then aged eighty-three who had worked underground, drawing with the belt and chain, as a girl, the practice must have continued in at least one pit until the 1870s. As for the employment of boys under ten, this was not effectively controlled until, after 1881, school attendance became compulsory and attendance officers – 'school-board men', as they were commonly called – were able to conduct an oblique attack on child labour. The considerable ingenuity that owners could employ to frustrate improvements in conditions is illustrated, quite late in the history of coal mining in Britain, by their manipulation of a 1911 requirement regarding pithead baths. This laid down that the employers must provide baths, to be maintained jointly by contributions from themselves and their employees, if a pithead ballot demanded them. Searching for a loophole to enable them to avoid this expense, the owners found that the demand was to be established by a majority in the ballot of 'two thirds of the workmen employed in any mine'. This, they argued, meant workmen employed underground; the others were employed *at*, not *in*, the mine. At the same time, the colliers' natural resistance to changing the habits of a lifetime was skilfully exploited, and their wives were persuaded that to end the domestic bathtime ritual would disrupt family life. Consequently, baths were built at only two pits in the five years after 1911, did not become at all common until the late 1930s, and in some coalfields – Somerset, for example – hardly existed until after nationalization in 1947. So in thousands of homes the living room continued to be converted – once, twice or three times a day, according to local shift practice and the number of colliers in the house – to a bathroom, with water heated over the range. What made this particularly absurd was that, since most winding was still by steam, the most expensive element in the provision of pithead baths, the hot-water supply, was freely available. Indeed, as early as 1840, as mentioned in an earlier chapter, the use of waste water from winding engines had been suggested for this purpose.

But it was in the sphere of safety that owners were at their most obstructive and apathetic. An Act of 1850 first provided for an inspectorate of mines although, as also noted earlier, its strength was pitiful and its powers limited. In 1855, it was necessary to strengthen and redefine the earlier safety regulations, and a further Act in 1860 added more controls. Bill draftsmen continued hard at work, producing the Act of 1862, making it mandatory to provide two shafts at every pit; of 1872, with more safety requirements; of 1886, providing for special inquiries into mining accidents; of 1887, of 1896, of 1903, of 1906, of 1910, of 1911 and of 1914. It might be thought that, after all this legislative fury, every possible loophole had been closed and every hazard banished, but in 1912 accidents still picked off 1276 miners, and in 1913, 1753, the increase being accounted for almost exactly by the toll of the Senghenydd disaster. This was a death rate, for 1913, of one in 713 men employed, and the likelihood in the same year of a man suffering an injury serious enough to put him off work for more than seven days was one in seven. (Comparable rates for 1980–81 were: fatalities thirty-nine, one in 7250; serious injuries – now defined as an injury serious enough to require admission to hospital for more than a day – 601, one in 470.) For all the British ingenuity and enterprise that had produced a technological revolution in the pits during the previous century, the death rate in the United

Kingdom's mines was, between 1907 and 1911, fourth among the eight leading coal-producing nations, and getting worse.

When, throughout the eighteenth and nineteenth centuries, demand for coal was growing, this had always been given as the excuse for poor safety standards and dangerous working practices. The coal trade peaked just before the First World War, and by 1925 it had slumped disastrously. In that year, 73 per cent of the coal was produced at a loss. If improvements in conditions could not be hoped for when times were good, they were unlikely to be made now. One bitter harvest of the years of neglect was an explosion that took place in 1934 and was – touch wood and discounting the obscene Aberfan tip slide of 1966 which was not, properly speaking, a mining accident – the last great pit disaster in Britain. The reason for examining the 1934 disaster in some detail (apart from the fact that it was the largest in the living memory of anyone under seventy) is that the events leading up to it, and the attitudes displayed during the subsequent inquiry, illustrate how little things had changed in the century since the first official inquiry had been made into safety in the pits. Moreover, in the economic blizzards of the 1920s and 1930s, whatever power the unions had had before 1914 had been overlaid as if it had never been.

The A483 road running southwest out of Chester into Clwyd is possibly the least interesting way into Wales. You hardly notice the bridge at Pulford that takes you across the border. A few miles further on, you come to a place called Gresford, an unremarkable main road settlement with its pub or two, a Spar store and a café, some filling stations. And then, when you've left the village behind and are watching for the outskirts of Wrexham, just before the roundabout you come across something incongruous.

It is a set of pithead gear made, it seems, out of giant Meccano. Nothing else. The buildings that used to surround it have been pulled down, and the spoil heaps have been bulldozed flat. The pit closed in November 1973, and on 9 December 1974 they cut the pithead cables and dropped them into the shaft. The pithead gear has been left standing as a memorial to the 260 or so colliers of northeast Wales who were working below on the morning of Saturday, 22 September 1934, and who are, most of them, still down there, blasted or burned into eternity by the explosion that occurred that morning at 2.08 a.m. precisely.

Gresford lies about halfway along the crescent of coal measures, fifty miles long and some six miles wide, that strikes inwards along the northeastern reaches of Wales from the Dee estuary through Flint and Mold, southwards under Wrexham and Ruabon to Oswestry. They started to dig for coal near Wrexham in the fifteenth century, at first working the outcrop down dip, and by the nineteenth all the most easily accessible coal had been brought out. From north to south, a mile or so west of Gresford, runs the Bala fault which drops the coal measures 400 yards deeper to the east. Only two pits have ever worked this lower area: Gresford, the first, and Llay Main, which opened in 1914 and closed in 1966.

They started to sink the Dennis shaft at Gresford in the spring of 1908, and the Martin, some 200 feet away, in the following year. It was March 1912 before sinking – complicated by running sand and drainage problems – was completed. Then the workforce built up quickly – there were 900 men at work by 1914 – and went on rising until, by the 1930s, it had increased to some 2200, of whom about 1850 worked underground.

The two shafts, Dennis and Martin, went down some 730 yards before they met the faulted Main Seam, between six and eight feet thick. Dennis carried men and coal, and took fresh air down. Martin handled men and supplies and brought stale air out. Up to about 1930, Gresford operated on nineteenth-century lines. The face was undercut and drilled for blasting, and the coal was loaded into twelve-hundredweight tubs which were hauled by horses to the pit bottom. It was a longwall pit. By 1934, coal cutters and conveyors had been introduced in some districts – an investment made in the interests of productivity despite the 'state of trade' which was the excuse for delaying the introduction of pit baths until 1939 and for a cheeseparing attitude to 'deadwork' – work that had nothing directly to do with the output of coal, but some of which might have prevented the 1934 disaster or at least reduced its toll.

Gresford was a fiery pit. It was 'red hot' according to one collier, for a fortnight before the explosion. Another, Edward Ponton, said of the area where the explosion occurred that it was 'very hot there, like hell'. After his first day's work in that area, William Duckworth got himself a larger drinking bottle and bought a couple of pairs of football shorts to work in, something he had never had to do before. Face-worker D. M. Lansley remembered nearly fifty years later that he used to take six pints of water on shift with him, drinking half of it as soon as he reached the face. As well as helping to cope with the heat and dust, the water had another advantage, he said: with that much water inside you, you didn't need to eat. As for gas, 'One could smell the explosion coming a few years before it actually happened, and it was in everyone's mind,' according to Mr Lansley. Collier John Hughes found that the gas made him feel 'very heavy and drowsy' when he got home, and he felt he did not want to go anywhere at all. Alfred Tomlinson said the gas made him sick and gave him a sore head; Leonard Price, too, reported 'bursting headaches'. Another Gresford man, R. E. Edwards, who was a fitter at the time of the explosion and took part in the rescue work, remembered that 'everyone who worked in the pit had the feeling that, some time, something serious was going to happen. The conditions down the pit, and the heat on working coalfaces, were unbearable. But we all had our jobs to do, and no one seemed to grumble; they just accepted it as normal conditions.'

The reason why they accepted it was simple: they had no choice. By the 1930s the morale of miners in Britain, betrayed over and over again even by their own political party, was at rock bottom. According to Mr Lansley, Gresford was still being worked by a charter-master system, though this must by 1934 have been a derivative, not a survival, of the charter-master system of the nineteenth century, which was synonymous with butty. 'The charter,' Mr Lansley recalled, 'was an ordinary coalface worker who was answerable to the management for his particular coalface, along with the fireman. It was the men under him who did the work, but he had the biggest pay packet just for being a yes-man.' I have to say that I have not come across any other reference to the charter-master system at Gresford, but it is certain that, whether for this or for other reasons, the Gresford workforce in the early 1930s was an embittered and resentful one, and there were certainly wide variations in pay.

There were three seams at Gresford: the Main, the Crank and the Brassey. By 1934, the Brassey was pretty well played out, and its men were gradually being transferred to the Main. The Main was worked in two sections, the Dennis and, some distance away – far enough away not to be affected by the explosion – the Southeast section. The Dennis section was, at its farthest extremes, over a mile from the bottom of the Dennis shaft. The way there started

with a flattish, not too uncomfortable walk along the Dennis main
road for about half a mile. Then you came to the clutch, the haulage
motor for the main section road, and turned half-left down a
one-in-nine slope. This road was called 142s Deep, and about 300
yards from the clutch you took a right turn into the first of the
Dennis districts or faces, known as 29s. After about another 500
yards there was another right turn into another district, 14s. Ahead
and to the left lay the other three Dennis districts, but it was the
29s, the 14s, and the area round the clutch that were to be
significant on the night of 22 September 1934.

The 14s face had been opened up at the beginning of 1934 and,
despite a series of roof falls in the spring, work had proceeded fast.
By September the face was advancing at the rate of seven yards a
week along a 200-yard front. It was a partly mechanized face;
indeed, in terms of the mining technology of the time, it was slap up
to date, and if its safety procedures had been equally well advanced
this chapter could not have been written. The coal was undercut by
a cutting machine, and was then brought down by blasting. It was
loaded by hand on to a belt conveyor which carried it to the tub
conveyor on 142s Deep, and so, via the clutch, to the Dennis shaft
bottom.

Conditions on 14s face in September 'could not', according to
one of the members of the inquiry into the disaster, 'be regarded as
satisfactory from any single standpoint'. As the face moved
forward, the space from which coal had been won was packed very
inadequately, and this was at least part of the cause of the
succession of roof falls. These falls had also restricted the supply of
fresh air, and only makeshift arrangements were made to make up
the deficit. The falls had also created cavities in which gas could
collect. So the 14s was being worked at a frenetic rate, beyond all
reason in terms of safe practice. The men working it were being
paid $22\frac{1}{2}$ per cent more per shift than those elsewhere in the
Dennis. Some of them, probably correctly, interpreted this as a
bonus for keeping their mouths shut, and to prevent their noses
from smelling gas and their heads from feeling dizzy.

The truth was that in 1934 Gresford Colliery was demoralized
from the top downwards. John Harrop, the company secretary, was
dying. William Bonsall, the manager, was left in sole charge of the
mine, without an agent with whom to discuss technical questions.
Bonsall was a Derbyshire man who had worked his way up from

haulage boy over forty-one years of pit experience. He had managed Gresford since 1917, but the agent who retired in 1932 had not been replaced, so that, as the inquiry report said, Bonsall was 'left to carry on the mine without the guidance of any technically informed superior official'. (The man who could have been called to account for this was Dyke Dennis, managing director of the United Westminster and Wrexham Collieries, but he did not give evidence.) There was certainly enough activity at Gresford – the intense concentration on the 14s face, the mechanization in progress in the Southeast section – for any staff shortage on the technical side to be severely felt, and it was said that because of Bonsall's preoccupation elsewhere he rarely visited the Dennis. The undermanager responsible for the Dennis was Andrew Williams, a man with thirty-eight years' experience, including nine as a manager and agent, but who had come to Gresford only that January. The fact that, with such previous experience, he had been prepared to take the undermanager's job may suggest some flaw in his background, but this was not brought out at the inquiry. Certainly, being an undermanager at Gresford was no sinecure. Andrew Williams customarily worked a twelve-and-a-half hour shift, and occasionally went back in the evening or during the night. He had, in fact, twice visited the night shift since his appointment. Of the three overmen, the next grade down, only one ever visited the Dennis – and that rarely – because he too was preoccupied with the mechanization of the Southeast section. This left the operation of the Dennis in the hands of deputies, of whom five were employed at night, one for each face.

The result of all this was that there were several gaps in the traditional chain of colliery command. The manager had his thoughts elsewhere. So did the overmen. The deputies, whose main job was to inspect the roads and workings to check the safety of roofs and walls, and to check the ventilation and test for gas, were also required, at Gresford, to supervise and in many instances actually do the shot-firing – setting off the controlled explosion which brought down the coal – itself a full-time job. In order to hold down their jobs, most men in positions of responsibility were doing more than they should, and it was not surprising that routine procedures were skimped or dispensed with. Plans to improve the ventilation were shelved in favour of the more productive work of pushing the faces onwards. Shot-firing was done in haste so as not to hold up the getting of coal. Even gas could not be allowed to get in the way of the coal, and compressed air was used as a quick way of dispersing it. This was within the law, and was not in itself dangerous, but it was certainly unwise since it solved the immediate problem without establishing the source. Compressed air was heavily used in 14s for this purpose. That 14s was a particularly gassy face was well known. Three months before the explosion, collier Alfred Tomlinson, on the afternoon shift, left his place on the face and made his way to a less hazardous spot. Harold Amos, the deputy, saw him and asked where he was going. 'Down to the big coal,' said Alfred Tomlinson. 'There are two boreholes here which want firing,' the deputy said. 'If you fire them you'll blow us all up to hell,' Tomlinson replied – but Amos fired all the same, and later denied that this conversation had taken place. The day-shift deputy, Jonathan Thomas, was equally imperturbable. William Melling, round about the same time, told him that 'there is a lot of stuff in here', meaning gas. 'It's not as bad as it has been,' was the reply.

The deputies were speaking for management, as most of them continued to do when they gave evidence to the inquiry. Even after some deputies' daily reports were discovered in the pit, where they should not have been, after the disaster, fifty-one reports for 1934 were still missing. They had either never been made, or they had been destroyed (as was widely believed locally), and it was not possible to decide which since some of them had been made, or not made, by the three deputies who died that Friday night, and the others by men whose answers were, at best, evasive. But record-keeping was not a strong point at Gresford. In June 1934, William Bonsall, the manager, told his assistant surveyor, William Cuffin, to stop the testing of the Dennis roads and faces for gas, despite the fact that this test was a legal requirement. The measurements for July and August subsequently found in Cuffin's notebook were imaginary. Bonsall came to him a day or two after the explosion and asked him to make them up. Some of this management slackness and deception might have been checked had the union been effective, but the North Wales Miners' Association was as demoralized as management. The joint union and management pit committee on safety does not seem to have functioned at all; perhaps it had no complaints to investigate, because, as Mr D. M. Lansley says bluntly, 'Every man down the pit was too frightened to make complaints about conditions because he knew that the boss would sack him, and although there was a union it had no power.' 'I am sorry to say it,' collier Ernest Parry told the Gresford inquiry, 'but this pit was not really a union pit, and all the complaints that I have known been taken to them, they have been ignored.'

The state of the records made it impossible after the explosion to establish the truth about the gas in 14s. Sir Herbert Walker, the chief inspector of mines who conducted the inquiry, heard a number of witnesses put up by the Miners' Association who declared that 'for several months before the explosion the occurrences of gas in 14s district were of a very grave character and that there were present frequently, if not almost continuously, at the top end of the face large bodies of gas in explosive proportions'. But he suspected that they were exaggerating, some unconsciously and some deliberately. It is likely that the Association, conscious after the explosion of its own sins of omission, was keen to deflect as much attention as possible to the sins of the management and in doing so overstated the case, and it is fairly clear that the Association had nothing to be proud of in its own record at Gresford.

There were nearly 500 men underground at Gresford on the night of Friday, 21 September. It was an abnormally large number, though many men from the afternoon shift habitually 'doubled through' the night so that they would not have to work on Saturday afternoon. Normally, the night shift was used for packing the spaces where coal had been taken, and for shifting the belt conveyors, but Friday nights was a coal-getting shift and, tragically as it turned out, that Friday night was especially busy in 29s face. 'Doubling through' was against the law, but William Bonsall said that 'many of the men liked it and asked for it'.

There were several particular reasons why even more men than usual were 'getting their six in' by working through the night. Wrexham was not a town normally rich in possibilities for entertainment, but that Saturday was to be an exception. It was the day of the annual Wrexham Carnival. Bertram Mills's Circus was in town. On top of that, Wrexham were playing Tranmere Rovers at home in a local derby. The Wrexham Colliery Silver Band was booked to play at the Racecourse ground, and some of its members doubled through for that reason. So it was an exceptionally heavy shift that walked through the pouring rain to the pithead that night, while many men underground eked out their water ration and prepared to work the night away.

Below, Harold Amos, the afternoon shift deputy on 14s, had had an irritating day. Going his round, he had found that a roof fall had left a cavity some ten inches deep, about two feet wide and four long. He tested for gas and found 2 per cent; the safe limit was reckoned to be a quarter of 1 per cent. With the shot-firer, Arthur Jones, Amos blew the gas out of the cavity with compressed air and bevelled the edge to let air flow into it. But the problem cleared itself up; making his last inspection round about nine o'clock that evening, he found the cavity clear. Arthur Jones, who had gone back to the spot earlier in the evening, found the same. But other men in 14s were later to say that there were large quantities of gas creeping down the face towards the end of the afternoon shift. William Duckworth – the man who worked in football shorts because it was so hot – found the gas so bad at the top end of the face that, at about eight o'clock, he moved down about eighty yards and worked on there until getting on for midnight.

When Arthur Jones came off shift at about eight o'clock there was another topic of conversation: a peculiar smell in the shaft. Frank Gibson, the onsetter, mentioned it to him when he reached the bank, and Arthur Jones said, 'Yes, someone has got their trousers down.' The smell persisted until Gibson went off at ten; it was, he said, 'a smell unlike anything he had smelled before or since', though his assistant did not notice it.

Other people had caught a strange smell – like dead mice, one man said – earlier that week. The smell was mentioned several times in evidence to the inquiry, and has also been mentioned by a number of former Gresford colliers in correspondence. 'You could smell trouble coming' is a typical comment. John Brass, the Yorkshire chartered engineer who was one of the assessors at the inquiry and who took a pro-management line, poured scorn on the reports of a smell. Some men said it was like an old sewer, others that it was like coal gas from the public supply. 'Firedamp has no smell such as was described,' he wrote – but then the human nose is a notoriously imprecise detection device, which is why Davy lamps and canaries were employed in the pits. Of course, the comments of my correspondents, writing in the mid-1970s, could be figurative, or they could have been influenced by the considerable local folklore which has built up round the disaster. The smell might have been, as Joseph Jones, Mr Brass's fellow assessor, suggested, the smell of a smouldering fire somewhere in the packing, and this might have been connected with the widely reported heat in the Dennis. The only other explanation is supernatural, and this, too, has its adherents.

The men came in that night, as many of them had done night after night for over twenty years, from Wrexham, Maesydre, Vron, Broughton and the other villages. Herbert Brain of Pentrefelin, thirty-one and a repairer of the pit roads, forced himself out even though he had been off sick with flu on the Wednesday and Thursday nights. On the other hand, Elijah Ellis of Rossett, waking with a headache, listened to his wife's advice and stayed at home. James Davies of Wrexham, twenty-one and a filler, was glad enough to be going to work; he had been off for three years and had started again only on Monday. Haulage hand Irwin Foulkes, twenty-one, kissed goodbye on his doorstep in Rhos to his bride of seven weeks and perhaps wished that things could have been otherwise.

Lamproom boy Albert Rowlands got to work early, running on ahead of his father. It was the job of the lamproom boys to collect the colliers' numbered tokens and hand out the correspondingly numbered lamps, the one check on who had actually turned up for work and gone below, and the source from which wage sheets (and on this occasion casualty lists) were prepared. The men came to the lamproom windows and exchanged their tokens for locked and lighted lamps. The more cautious turned their flames down to check that they could, in fact, be turned low in case of gas. One or two handed their lamps back, asking for the wicks to be drawn lower. Then, sixteen at a time, they waited for the cages. It was about ten o'clock, and there were about four hours left for 260 men of Gresford.

Below, tending his stationary engine, 'Little Jackie' Cartwright had planned to double through. His father was off sick with heart trouble, the family needed the money from Jackie's six shifts, and Jackie himself was looking forward to his free Saturday at the Carnival. He was a midget, only four feet three inches tall. 'Though his body was a normal size,' his sister Gwyneth remembers, 'his arms and legs were short, though powerful.' He had other attributes: he was ambidextrous, something rare enough to make him special in Gresford, and he was a happy extrovert, much in demand as a performer for local charities.

What happened to 'Little Jackie' that Friday night defies explanation, but it is well attested from more than one source – he died from hereditary heart disease in 1974, and was buried on the day that they cut the shaft ropes at Gresford and cast them down – in the conviction that he had been a brand plucked from the burning. At ten o'clock, as the men who were not doubling through went off afternoon shift, Jackie Cartwright heard a voice. 'I had an awful feeling that something was wrong,' he said later. 'I could hear something saying to me, "Jackie, go home." I said to my mates, "Let's go home, lads. I'm going anyway" – and they laughed at me and called me a big baby.' But he took his lamp and ran, reaching the pit bottom just in time to catch the last cage up.

It must have been midnight when he reached home. The house was locked for the night, the family asleep. His father came down to let him in in answer to his knocks, and Jackie lied that the cutter had broken down. Gwyneth Cartwright, then twelve, remembers hearing the conversation downstairs: 'My mam got up and went downstairs and got Jackie a meal and hot water for his bath.' It was Saturday, and the fuse of the Gresford timebomb was alight. 'I believe,' Gwyneth adds as a postscript to Jackie's story, 'that the rescuers got within sight of Jackie's engine, the other side of the fire doors, and it was white hot.'

Meanwhile, in the lamproom, the rush was over. Albert Rowlands and his mates of six weeks settled to the routine of cleaning and trimming the lamps out of the afternoon shift, and filling them ready for the next day. Outside, the rain was falling vertically, and an autumn night settled heavily over Gresford. The lamps done, Albert lay back on the cleaning bench, dozing. One or two others dragged lazily on their Woodbines, proud emblems of employment. Below in the Dennis district, in 29s and 14s and the other faces, the men of Gresford cut and filled, swigged water, and planned their Saturdays. A collier's job is one for a beast; it does not fill your mind, so colliers have time to think, plan, even dream. There were men who were going to the match, and some were looking for better play from Frewin and Snow, who had been off form lately. Some men – not many – would be at the prizegiving ceremony of the Juvenile Order of Rechabites Temperance Society at Brymbo. Others were looking forward to taking the family to Bertram Mills to see the Ross Mechanical Man and Jeanette's Cricketing Elephants. For some, it would be two seats in the back row of the Empire or the Hippodrome.

At eight minutes past two, Gresford blew up. Overman Frederick Davies was in his cabin near the bottom of the Dennis shaft, the most senior man on shift. At first, he thought a cage had crashed down the shaft, and went to look. Before he had taken more than a few steps he was enveloped in dust. Turning back, he telephoned the banksman with orders to fetch William Bonsall and Andrew Williams at once. 'Something has happened down the Dennis,' he said. 'I think it has fired.' Then he told haulage driver Edward Williams to phone the clutch, but there was no answer. The earpiece was hanging from its hook by the cord, and near it was the body of Alex Palmer, a 20-year-old haulage hand.

Dai Jones was the night-shift deputy in 29s district. He was near the face when there was a noise that he thought sounded like a burst compressed-air pipe. A second later he was blown off his feet in a hail of dust and stones. Jack Samuel was nearby, waiting for his cutting machine to be moved up. 'What the hell's up, Jack?' said his brother Albert when they heard the noise. Jack said, 'That's the bloody bottom gone,' meaning 14s district. They moved – fast – and tripped over Dai Jones. Dai said, 'Jack, your air pipes are burst.' 'Don't talk soft,' said Jack, who was about to demonstrate more leadership than had been seen at Gresford for a long time. 'Come on Dai, the bottom's gone.'

Their district, 29s, was the last on the Dennis section to receive the flow of air from the Dennis shaft to the Martin. Access to the face was normally by way of the haulage road, the best part of a mile, to a point on 142s Deep – the Dennis's main road – known as 29s turn. But that would have meant walking into the air flow and into any trouble – fire, gas or dust – it might be carrying along from 14s. Jack's idea was for them to make their way with the air, up one of the old wind roads. As they moved along the face they came across a group of men who were 'rather excited' and wanted to know what had happened. Jack told them to keep calm and follow him. The first wind road they tried was too full of dust, but they picked up a few more men there. By now, the party was about seventy strong, with Dai Jones bringing up the rear and Jack in the lead with another collier, Robert Andrews.

The next wind road, Old 99s as it was called, was clearer and they set off along it. After about 400 yards, Robert Andrews found a man's body. He and Jack linked hands and pulled him out from a side road and tried to revive him, but he was too far gone. Then Robert Andrews fell over. Dai Jones's nerve was going. He rushed from the back of the party, not saying a word, and was going to get ahead on his own. 'I collared him by the shoulder,' Jack said later. 'I told him not to be a damn fool and to take his time. He came back.'

They went on, and came to a door. Pushing it open a few inches, they caught a warm wind and a smell of burning. As they stood wondering what to do one of the party, cutting machineman Bill Crump, said that there were some more doors further up; if they could get beyond those, they would be all right.

'We called to the other men,' Jack Samuel's story goes on, 'and told them what we were going to do and told them to get anything they had – caps, singlets or anything to fan with, and to follow close together. We put Dai Jones, the deputy, down on his hands and knees and Fisher took the lead.' This was Thomas Fisher, a collier. 'We kept wafting these bits of rag and our caps and things round our faces. It was very hot and a lot of gas there.' Dai Jones said he was done for, but Jack urged him on, and they came to a ladder. By now most of the men had either turned back or fallen behind, and there were Jack, his brother Albert, Dai Jones, Thomas Fisher, Robert Andrews and Cyril Challoner left.

'The going had been heavy and it was hot, and Dai Jones again said he was done. Fisher and Challoner had started up the ladder by this time, and I said to my brother, "Take your time. Don't be in a hurry. We'll not leave Dai here." We got him to the foot of the ladder and he got his hands on the rungs and I got my shoulder underneath him and pushed him up. As we were going up the ladder he seemed to revive and the air was clearer.'

They had climbed seventy feet across a fault to the return airway. Part of the time, they went on their hands and knees, with three lamps between them. For a while, they made good headway, but then Robert Andrews started to flag. Dai Jones, Albert Samuel and Cyril Challoner were ahead, but Jack called Thomas Fisher back, saying, 'Take your time. We'll not leave Andrews behind if we have to carry him.' He called to the others to wait, and while he and Fisher were helping Andrews along to catch up, 'there came a big gush of wind down the road and I said, "Thank God, they've reversed the wind. We're all right now. Let's get this way as soon as we can now." And we continued out against the wind along this junction road and we came to a man who was dead and then we carried on a bit further and I heard my brother shout "We're by the clutch." '

They carried on over falls and runaway tubs until they met Andrew Williams, the undermanager, and fitter Tom Tilston, one of the rescue party. This was not to be known for another forty hours, but the six men led by Jack Samuel were the only men on shift in the Dennis section to survive.

A full-scale rescue attempt was by now getting under way. Andrew Williams and William Bonsall had reached the pit by about 2.30 a.m. The first thing that lamp boy Albert Rowlands had known of something amiss was when someone thumped on the lamproom door shouting 'Something's wrong, they're coming up!' 'Some time passed,' Mr Rowlands remembered in 1976, 'and then out they came, from another area of the pit, not knowing anything, not saying anything, just handing in their lamps and heading home or just hanging around.' His father was below, and he was never going to see him again. Meanwhile, Albert was sent on his bike to round up the first-aid and rescue men from Wrexham. The rescue team at the nearby Llay Main Colliery, three of whose members were to die, had already been alerted.

One of the men Albert Rowlands knocked up that night was Tom Tilston, whom Jack Samuel's party had met on their way out. He was one of the first to arrive, and went down in the cage with Andrew Williams. At the pit bottom, things seemed normal, but as they approached the clutch they met falls of rock. Jack Samuels told them about the seventy or so men they had left behind, and so Tom Tilston and Andrew Williams tried to retrace Jack's steps down the wind road. It was not long before the canary they were carrying went down, and so they returned and went down the main road towards 29s turn. There, Tom Tilston remembered, 'We were met by fire, everything that would burn being alight, including pit props and tubs of coal, the whole scene being one of destruction.'

Electrician W. L. Hayward had been near the Dennis shaft when he heard the explosion. It knocked him to the ground; when he opened his eyes he could see nothing for dust. He found Frederick Davies, the overman, who told him to try to repair the phone lines; but there was not enough new cable and Hayward gave up. On his way back to the pit bottom he met a rescue party, one of whose lamps had gone out. Hayward handed over his own, and shortly afterwards went off duty since there was nothing more he could do. Two days later, he was to see his name on a list of the dead posted in a Wrexham shop. 'When I met my mates in town,' he said later, 'they couldn't believe their eyes. They asked was it me and when I assured them that it was they rushed around me, shaking my hand and patting my back.' 'Little Jackie' Cartwright was another who was rumoured to have been killed, as he certainly would have been had he stayed at his post, though his name was not on the official list. He found that when he went into Wrexham people treated him with unusual reserve. 'They thought they were seeing a ghost, such was the atmosphere around the district,' his sister Gwyneth remembers.

The fire at 29s turn was now being fought by a party which included Tom Tilston. It was a hopeless struggle. The six-inch compressed air main had broken and the air was fanning the fire. There was no water supply, and there was a grievous shortage of firefighting equipment, even of sand and fire extinguishers, and the men were reduced to trying to smother the flames with dirt and dust off the road. The falls in the Dennis main road prevented more supplies being brought in, except by hand, and parties of colliers were set to clear them. It took them until five on the Saturday evening to clear the road, but by that time the fire was spreading back to the pit bottom.

By dawn, the first bodies had been brought up the Dennis shaft. John Williams, captain of the Llay Main rescue team, was resting with his men in the general office at the pit bank when a call came for the full team of six to go below. As it happened, one man's breathing set was not working, so he stayed behind. The return airway, along which Jack Samuel had made his escape, was now believed to be clear of gas, and William Bonsall had given orders for the rescue men to go in and test it, but to wait until he was there. The second part of this instruction was not relayed to the men, or to the deputy on the spot, Harold Thomas.

When the rescue party reached the pit bottom, another breathing set was found to be out of order. The sets had not been tested, contrary to regulations, and subsequent inspection of the rescue equipment in general in the Wrexham area showed much of it to be defective or obsolete, or both. So in the event four men of the rescue team – John Williams, Bill and Dan Hughes and Jack

Lewis – went into the airway with Harold Thomas, who was carrying the canary. The bird went down when they had got five or six yards in, and John Williams told the deputy to go back.

It remains a complete mystery why the rescue men, too, did not turn back. The death of the canary only a few yards from the airway entrance meant that no one further in could have survived. John Williams, however, got the men together and told them that there was a probability that there were still men alive in there, and they decided to go on, with Williams in the lead and the others spaced out at intervals of about twenty yards. After about 200 yards the air got hotter and there was a blockage. Williams signalled to the others to halt, and himself backed down the airway because, wearing his breathing set, he had no room to turn round. 'I turned back,' he told the inquiry, 'took the first man I came to, Bill Hughes, back on to Jack Lewis, and took those two on to Dan Hughes, and told them the conditions: that we were done; we had better get back.' To speak to them, it was necessary to push the mouthpiece of the breathing set to one side. To have done this, Sir Henry Walker wrote in the inquiry report, was 'suicidal, and the extraordinary thing is that Williams himself survived'.

He was the only one to do so. Jack Lewis and Bill Hughes seemed to panic, ignoring Williams's shout to take their time. In the rush to get out, Jack Lewis was the first to fall. John Williams found him already dead, with his breathing apparatus still working. Then Bill Hughes fell dead and Dan staggered on, failing fast. John Williams caught up with him and helped him along, holding him up and pushing him forward, until Williams fell on top of Hughes. Finding that the feed pipe from his oxygen cylinder had disconnected itself – probably in his struggle to keep Dan Hughes going – Williams stuffed the pipe in his mouth. Dan was still alive – 'on his knees, crumpled up, but alive', according to Williams – and lights could be seen at the top end of the airway, perhaps fifty yards away. Williams called, and someone whistled. He called again, and waited for what seemed like four or five minutes. No one came, so he made his own way out, leaving Dan Hughes behind. They brought Dan Hughes's body out some hours later.

At the Cartwrights' house, there had been a furious knocking on the door at about 7.30 on the Saturday morning. It was a friend of Jackie's, asking after him and giving his parents their first news of the disaster. Gwyneth Cartwright, as she then was, remembers that breakfast-time: 'When Jackie came downstairs, my dad told my mam to say nothing about it, and then after breakfast he told Jackie the news.' Jackie got up from the table, stood with his back to the fire and made his confession, with tears, as Gwyneth remembers, running down his cheeks. Breakfast was unusual that morning at the home of Mrs Percy Rogers, whose husband's family worked a smallholding over Gresford pit at Acton. Mrs Rogers's bachelor brother had come to stay there on Friday night, bringing his whippet, which slept in a kennel close to the house. In the morning the dog was found to be missing. The dog was eventually found at home, over two miles away, sitting trembling by the back door, having jumped or scrambled over the high backyard door of the Rogers's house. It was concluded that it must have heard the explosion, or perhaps felt it, and fled.

In Wrexham, as news of the disaster spread, the town was stunned. R. E. Edwards heard the news as he cycled in to work from Brymbo: 'Gresford's blown up!' people shouted. He took no notice, but travelled on to the pit, where he found that it was true enough: 'When I got to the works yard, it was alive with people.' There was a call for volunteers, so he collected a lamp and went down. For the next six hours he worked nonstop, carting sand to quench the fire at 29s turn and then fixing up a pipeline from the pit bottom up the Dennis shaft, in the hope of draining off the gas. Meanwhile, in the town, Bertram Mills's Circus decided not to open, and instead took down its big top and departed, leaving behind a 100-guinea cheque for the relief fund which, by Saturday midday, had already been opened. The Wrexham *v.* Tranmere football match went ahead, collections there providing a useful contribution to the fund, but the colliery band did not play as planned, and some of its members would never play again. All local amateur soccer was cancelled. The carnival went ahead as planned, but Wrexham's heart wasn't in it and some youths who tried to liven things up by giving girls the 'bumps' and stuffing confetti down their necks were roughly handled, in some cases by the girls themselves. Up at Gwersyllt Hill, the life of John Harrop, sixty-eight, secretary of the Gresford Colliery, was fading away. He had been ill for some weeks, and he died on the Sunday without knowing of the disaster that had overtaken the pit. Messages began to arrive: from the King and Queen at Balmoral, from Stanley Baldwin, from Lloyd George, from mayors of neighbouring towns.

On Saturday evening, the relief fund committee met for the first time.

Down below, the fire at 29s turn – or rather, the fire which had been at 29s turn, but which was steadily advancing towards the pit bottom – was still being fought by volunteer crews, working in relays of two hours. Tom Tilston, who had gone home at midday, was back by six in the evening. 'Twenty men would be called for,' said the Gresford managing director, Dyke Dennis, 'and one hundred would come forward.' The editor of the *Wrexham Advertiser* made a midnight visit to the pithead on Saturday. 'The numbers,' he wrote, 'had dwindled and none but those engaged on the essential services, and the relatives who kept a vigil that none could break, remained at the pithead. Despite the bitter wind that pierced with gale force to the very bone, women with infants in their arms waited, watched and hoped and never could be deterred from either.'

At this stage the official line was still that there might have been as many as 100 men trapped, and the fiction was being maintained that good progress was being made with firefighting and that, perhaps by Sunday afternoon, the fire could be put out. 'I realize now,' Albert Rowlands said in 1976, 'that rescuers who had dared to approach that wall of flame must have known the fate of anyone behind it.' Someone who suspected the true scale of the disaster was the *Daily Mail* reporter Don Iddon, then at the beginning of a distinguished career, who got a scoop by looking into the lamproom and guessing at the number of empty spaces on the shelves.

On Sunday, sightseers arrived, delayed in their journey by RAC patrolmen on the road from Chester, who stopped all non-essential traffic and collected £174 for the relief fund. The Salvation Army turned up at the pithead, playing 'O God our Help in Ages Past' and other appropriate hymn tunes. Rescue men brought out the body of George Roberts, a 28-year-old filler, the last, as it turned out, to be recovered. Then, as darkness fell, the rescue teams were suddenly recalled from the pit, Sir Henry Walker, chief inspector of mines, being the last to emerge. He, the company directors and union officials disappeared into a meeting which lasted for an hour and a half. 'The look on the faces of those representatives,' reported the *Wrexham Advertiser*, 'told us the result. It was the end.' The statement was posted up at 7.45 p.m. The fire had won, and was spreading. Further explosions had been heard beyond it, deep in the Dennis. The gas was so heavy in the return airways that no one could still be alive. It had been decided to abandon the pit and seal the shaft with 254 men of Gresford still down there. 'Slowly the relatives were persuaded to break their vigil and be led home, knowing that it was the last farewell to those men,' the *Wrexham Advertiser* reported. Henry Peters of Llay, thirty, a packer, left a widow and nine children; so did 59-year-old repairer John Tarran of Buckley. Three Clutton brothers – John, thirty-five, Arthur, twenty-nine, and 20-year-old George – died. So did the three Nicholas brothers, Harry, John and William, roughly the same ages. Robert Thomas's widow had five children, aged between nine and two and a half, to bring up. The Ministry of Health made haste to remind dependants claiming relief that they must take with them to the office the victims' medical cards, with their marriage certificates and the children's birth certificates, though 'if these were not available no expense should be incurred in obtaining them'. Albert Rowlands would spend the next few days 'in a dream, from home, to the pit, to my grandmother's, always wondering "How long can they live down there?"' Gwyneth Cartwright knew a widow who went on, for days, preparing her husband's meals and warming his clean clothes. By Sunday evening, trucks bringing in timber and corrugated iron and cement to seal the Dennis were signalling the end, though the end had, in truth, come about an hour after the explosion when the fire at 29s turn took hold.

But Gresford had one more victim still to claim. On Tuesday, 25 Setpember, round about 1.30 p.m., the sealing operations were being completed. A policeman on duty at the pithead was taking a break in a brick hut about thirty yards from the shaft and noticed the walls shaking. 'Harness was hanging on hooks,' he said later, 'and it began to jump about. The next moment I heard two deep, fearful rumblings.' The Dennis was exploding again. 'I had just made up my mind to run when a great spiral of smoke began shooting up from the downshaft,' the policeman went on. 'I did run, and it was a good job. Within three seconds there was a terrific roar. I turned round and saw the whole of the fan house shattered. Everything of the building was cleared from the surface and there was one big gaping hole.' A further blast followed a few minutes later; Gresford, it seemed was going mad. It had certainly taken another life, that of surface worker John Smith, who was snatched up by the blast, hurled about thirty yards and then showered with debris.

They opened the inquiry into Gresford on 25 October. It was a distinguished gathering, which included Sir Stafford Cripps, appearing for the Miners' Association, Mr (as he then was) Hartley Shawcross, a future Attorney-General, representing the colliery company, and the veteran miners' leader Peter Lee, of the Mineworkers' Federation of Great Britain. (It was Peter Lee's last contribution to the welfare of miners; he died before the inquiry report was completed.) The inquiry sat for thirty-eight days and heard evidence from 189 witnesses, who did not, however, include Dyke Dennis nor his sons, Pat and Vic, the effective directors of the United Westminster and Wrexham Collieries. It was left to William Bonsall to accept full responsibility, and he was found guilty of fourteen different breaches of the law relating to pit safety.

Members of the inquiry were not, of course, able to inspect the pit, which remained sealed for six months and, for some time after that, was only entered by trained specialists. Nor did they have any eyewitnesses to question. The only survivors from the Dennis was Jack Samuel's group of six men, and they could tell only of effects, not causes. Not surprisingly, opinion divided on the cause of the blast. Sir Stafford Cripps, for the miners, thought that an accumulation of gas on the 14s face had been exploded by something like a spark from a cutter, an accident with a lamp or a misfired shot. W. J. Charlton, divisional inspector of mines, representing the Mines Department of the Board of Trade, put the cause of the explosion at the clutch. His theory was that men working near the clutch had been alerted to a build-up of gas, and that when they retreated to the cabin to telephone a warning the phone, which was not of the safety pattern, sparked off the explosion. 'When the man turned the handle to give the signal,' said Mr Charlton, 'he blew that pit up.' For the colliery company, Hartley Shawcross had another possibility to suggest, and it was an ingenious one not well informed by mining technology, but cleverly placing the blame for the 265 deaths of their comrades on the Gresford colliers themselves. The trouble went back, Mr Shawcross said, to 1926, the year of the General Strike. When work was stopped in that year, a pillar of coal had been left and it had remained unworked since. Gas had leaked into this abandoned working, and at the same time the pillar – the pillar of the colliers' own making, because they had struck instead of working it – had heated up. If this were so, 'You would ultimately get flame which would ignite the surrounding area of gas, which together with the gas generated by distillation in the course of the heating itself would be ample to create the damage which was in fact done by the explosion which occurred.'

Well, perhaps it didn't matter much who was right. There were 166 widows to think about, as well as 229 orphaned children. Of the victims, 153 were in their twenties and thirties. Management standards at Gresford had become so decayed that there was little to be learned by specific example. Wherever the blast had occurred, it had been made more likely, perhaps inevitable, by failures of management, of record-keeping, of routine safety precautions and checks, even of the maintenance of rescue apparatus in good repair. But Percy Dominy, the inspector of mines responsible for Gresford (and for forty-five other pits – staffing in the inspectorate was still parsimonious), had not been seriously worried by these failures, some of which he had observed. It is probable that Gresford was no worse and no better than many other British pits in the 1930s. By luck more than judgement, the others managed to avoid disasters of such proportions.

They held a memorial service on 30 September 1934 at Wrexham Parish Church, as they have done on the nearest Sunday ever since. They started with 'Abide with me', followed by the first sentences of the burial service and the Twenty-third Psalm. It was right to include the burial service; there were still 254 men below ground who would never be buried in the conventional sense, but whose burial had begun with scamped deputy's reports and the turning of deaf ears to complaints. The lesson was from I Corinthians 15, thirty-eight verses of it: 'We shall not all sleep, but we shall all be changed. In a moment, in the twinkling of an eye, at the last trump; for the trumpet shall sound, and the dead shall be raised incorruptible, and we shall be changed. . . . O death, where is thy sting? O grave, where is thy victory? . . . Be ye steadfast, unmoveable, always abounding in the work of the Lord, forasmuch as ye know that your labour is not in vain in the Lord.'

No one ever went back into the Dennis section. Six months after the explosion, the work of unsealing the shafts and reopening Gresford began. The Dennis section and its 254 victims were sealed off. Thomas Tudor and Tom Tilston went to London to sing in the West End theatres in aid of the disaster fund. To the distress of the widows and orphans of Gresford was added the misery of the 2000 or so survivors of the disaster thrown out of work by the closure of the pit. Jackie Cartwright was one of them. 'After being out of work for eighteen months,' his sister remembers, 'Jackie had tried everywhere to get a job and finally returned to work at Gresford.' This was early in 1936, when production was slowly resumed. Jackie was to work on there until 1963, ten years before the pit closed for good. It was in the spring of 1937 that the colliery company, William Bonsall, Andrew Williams and various lesser management figures came to court, faced with a number of charges. Eight of these stuck, and the fines totalled £140. The price of a collier's life turned out to have gone up since Senghenydd in 1913. It was, in 1934, just over ten shillings. Perhaps that was progress.

Appendix

MAP OF GRESFORD COLLIERY

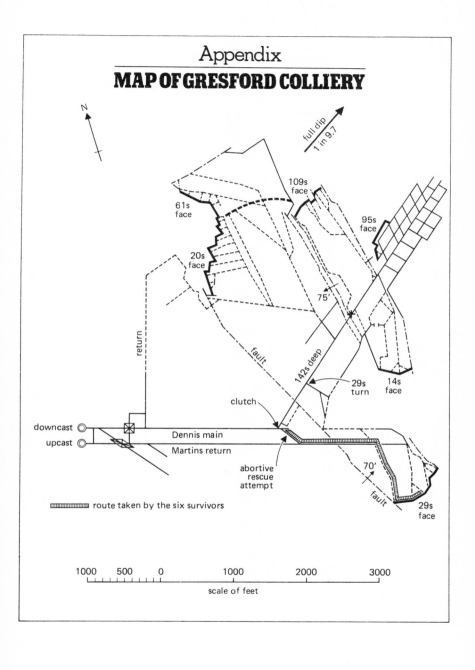

N

full dip 1 in 9.7

109s face

61s face

95s face

20s face

75'

142s deep

fault

return

29s turn

14s face

clutch

downcast

upcast

Dennis main

Martins return

abortive rescue attempt

70'

fault

29s face

route taken by the six survivors

1000   500   0   1000   2000   3000

scale of feet

BIBLIOGRAPHY

The basis of this book has been the huge corpus of Parliamentary papers
on the subject of coal mining, and in particular:

'Children's Employment Commission, First Report: Mines' and 'Appen-
dix of Evidence', 1842
'Coal Mines Act', 1911
'Inspectors of Mines Reports'
'Midland Mining Commission, First Report: South Staffordshire', 1843
'Royal Commission on the Coal Industry', report of 1919
'Royal Commission on the Coal Industry', report of 1926
'Royal Commission on Explosions from Coal Dust in Mines', reports,
1891–94
'Royal Commission on Mines', reports, 1907–11
'Select Committees on Accidents in Coal Mines', reports of 1835, 1849,
1853, 1854, 1811, 1886

The following books have proved generally helpful:

Ashton, T. S. and Sykes, J., *The Coal Industry of the Eighteenth Century*, 2nd
revised edition, Manchester: University Press, 1964
Bulman, H. F., *Coal Mining and the Coal Miner*, London: Methuen, 1920
Dickie, J. P., *The Coal Problem*, London: Methuen, 1936
Duckham, Helen and Baron, *Great Pit Disasters*, Newton Abbot: David
and Charles, 1973
Jevons, H. Stanley, *British Coal Trade*, London: Kegan Paul, 1915
Nef, J. U., *The Rise of the British Coal Industry*, London: Routledge, 1932
Simonin, L., *Underground Life, or Mines and Miners*, trans. and ed.,
Bristow, H. W., London: Chapman and Hall, 1869

ACKNOWLEDGEMENTS

Individuals, organizations and sources to whom I am grateful for help with specific points of detail are acknowledged chapter by chapter below. For more general help, I am deeply grateful to the National Coal Board Library, the London Library, Clwyd County Library Local History Section and the Swaffham Branch of Norfolk County Library.

Introduction

Harold Nicolson and George V are quoted from Harold Nicolson, *King George V, His Life and Reign*, London: Constable, 1952.

Chapter 1

The Carlyle quotations are from *Signs of the Times* (1829), and Defoe is quoted from *A Tour Through the Whole Island of Great Britain* (1726). For information on Hamilton Palace I am indebted to Anna Sproule, *Lost Houses of Britain*, Newton Abbot: David and Charles, 1982. Mr D. M. Lansley on conditions at Gresford Colliery is quoted from personal correspondence, and Mr R. E. Edwards from Roy Palmer, *Poverty Knock*, Cambridge: Cambridge University Press, 1974. Information on pit closures in the north Somerset coalfield is from C. G. Down and A. J. Warrington, *The History of the Somerset Coalfield*, Newton Abbott: David and Charles, 1971, and on closures in South Wales from Graham Humphrys, *Industrial Britain: South Wales*, Newton Abbot: David and Charles, 1972. The comments on the contemporary lifestyles of Grimethorpe miners are from Graham Turner, 'The Changing Lifestyle of our Miners', *Sunday Telegraph*, 14 November 1982. Jeremy Bugler on Cambois is from Roger Vielvoye *et al.*, *Coal: Technology for Britain's Future*, London: Macmillan, 1976.

Chapter 2

I am obliged to Tom and Sally North for making available to me the diary quoted at the beginning of this chapter. Information on the Bewick family pit at Mickley Common is from *A Memoir of Thomas Bewick written by Himself*, 1862 (modern edition, Oxford: Oxford University Press, 1975), and on ironmaking developments at Coalbrookdale from W. K. V. Gale, *Iron and Steel*, London: Longmans, 1969. For the comment on pillar-robbing in Fife I am indebted to H. J. Parry, 'Coping with Fife's Mining Industrial Heritage', *Municipal Engineer*, July/August, 1983. Information on nineteenth-century investment in the northeast and the later career of Sir George Elliott is from Norman McCord, *Northeast England*, London: Batsford, 1979. For details of developments in the Castleford and Pontefract area, and of the early exploration of the Selby coalfields, I have drawn on my own contribution to *Coal: Technology for Britain's Future*, London: Macmillan, 1976. The history of Ridings Pit, Stanton Drew, is from C. G. Down and A. J. Warrington, *The History of the Somerset Coalfield*, Newton Abbott: David and Charles, 1971. The reference to Dick the Devil is from Jon Raven, *The Folklore of Staffordshire*, London: Batsford, 1978, and those to other mythical colliers from A. L. Lloyd, *Folksong in England*, London: Lawrence and Wishart, 1967. The description of Bob Towers is from the BBC Radio programme 'The Big Hewer', produced by Charles Parker. The George Orwell references are from Sonia Orwell and Ian Angus, eds., *The Collected Essays, Journalism and Letters of George Orwell, Volume 1*, London: Martin Secker and Warburg, 1968.

Chapter 3

J. L. and Barbara Hammond are quoted from their book *The Town Labourer*, 4th revised edition, London: Longmans Green, 1925, and Frederick Engels from *The Condition of the Working Class in England in 1844*, London: Swan Sonnenschien, 1892. Tom Mann is quoted from his *Memoirs*, London: The Labour Publishing Company, 1923. The Edinburgh coalmaster quoted is R. Bald, *A General View of the Coal Trade of Scotland*, Edinburgh, 1808. Information on the guss and crook is from the 'Report of the Guss Committee', London: HMSO, 1928. The sceptical historian quoted is L. C. B. Seaman; *Victorian England: Aspects of English and Imperial History*, London: Methuen, 1973.

Chapter 4

The mid-nineteenth century writer quoted on comparisons between pit villages and manufacturing towns is from Barrie Trinder, *The Making of the*

Industrial Landscape, London: Dent, 1982. Information on the early days of Methodism is from Rupert E. Davies, *Methodism*, London: Epworth Press, 1953 and from John Wesley's *Journals*. The anti-Methodist hymn parody is quoted from Jon Raven, *The Urban and Industrial Songs of the Black Country and Birmingham*, Wolverhampton: Broadside, 1977. *The Gentleman's Magazine*, 1739, is quoted from John Pudney, *John Wesley*, London: Thames and Hudson, 1978. Memories of Flockton in the mid-1860s are from Kenneth Young, *Chapel*, London: Eyre Methuen, 1972. The story of illicit distilling in Newcastle is from Norman McCord, *Northeast England*, London: Batsford, 1979. The Reverend Henry Worsley is quoted from his *Juvenile Depravity*, London: Gilpin, 1849. The 'pills for all ailments' advertisement appeared in the *Wrexham Advertiser*, 27 September 1934. The story of Ruff Moey is from *The Urban and Industrial Songs of the Black Country and Birmingham, op. cit.* The critics of theatres as moral hazards are quoted from Geoffrey Pearson, *Hooligan, A History of Respectable Fears*, London: Macmillan Press, 1983, and the examples of playbills from Robert Wood, *Entertainments 1800–1900*, London: Evans, 1971.

Chapter 5

The *Newcastle Journal* of 1767 is quoted from J. L. and Barbara Hammond, *The Town Labourer*, 4th revised edition, London: Longmans Green, 1925. The visit of King George V and Queen Mary to the South Wales and Yorkshire coalfields is described in Harold Nicolson's *King George V: His Life and Reign*, London: Constable, 1952. I am obliged to Norman Voake for verifying the reference to the memorial stone in Midsomer Norton churchyard and the circumstances of the accident which it commemorates. Information on the overwinding accident at Pensford in 1944 and on the events at New Rock Colliery in 1957 is from C. G. Down and A. J. Warrington, *The History of the Somerset Coalfield*, Newton Abbott: David and Charles, 1972.

Chapter 6

Information on the Brora Colliery is from 'Highland Coal Mine', *Industrial Archaeology*, February 1969. The 1811 description of colliers on binding day is from *A Historical and Descriptive View of the County of Northumberland*, Newcastle: Mackenzie and Dent, 1811. Lord Londonderry is quoted from Sydney and Beatrice Webb, *The History of Trade Unions*, London: Longmans, 1920. The correspondent quoted on charter masters at Gresford Colliery in 1934 is Mr D. M. Tansley. For information on the free miners of the Forest of Dean I am indebted to

Cyril E. Hart, *The Free Miners*, Gloucester: The British Publishing Company, 1953; H. G. Nicholls, *The Forest of Dean*, London: John Murray, 1858; and Brian Waters, *The Forest of Dean*, London: Dent, 1951. I am obliged to Mr W. H. Biggs of Radstock for information about the Marsh Lane pit, Farrington Gurney, and to the *Somerset Guardian* for putting me in touch with him.

Chapter 7

Harold Nicolson is quoted from *King George V: His Life and Reign*, London: Constable,1952. Information on relations between Sir Oswald Mosley and Arthur Cook is from Nicholas Mosley, *Rules of the Game*, London: Secker and Warburg, 1982, and the Webbs on Alexander Macdonald is from Sydney and Beatrice Webb, *The History of Trade Unions*, London: Longmans, 1920. Beatrice Webb on the Derbyshire miners is from Norman and Jeanne Mackenzie, eds., *The Diary of Beatrice Webb, Volume 2: 1892–1905*, London: Virago, 1983. The note on the spitting habits of Northumberland miners is from *A Historical and Descriptive View of the County of Northumberland*, Newcastle: Mackenzie and Dent, 1811, and J. L. and Barbara Hammond are quoted from *The Town Labourer*, 4th revised, London: Longmans Green, 1925. John Williams is quoted from George Ewart Evans, *From Mouths of Men*, London: Faber, 1976. I am indebted to the late A. L. Lloyd for information on the South Medomsley strike and the Durham lockout. On the Durham Miners' Gala I have drawn from John Mappledeck, 'Banners and Bands at the Big Meeting', *Listener*, 21 July, 1983; Roy Kerridge, 'Taffies and Geordies', *Spectator*, 23 July, 1983; and Michael Nally, 'Pit Closure Fears will Cloud Gala', *Observer*, 26 June, 1983. Information on the Dunkerton carting boys' strike is from C. G. Down and A. J. Warrington, *The History of the Somerset Coalfield*, Newton Abbott: David and Charles, 1971.

Chapter 8

Accident statistics for 1980–81 are from 'National Coal Board Report and Accounts, 1980–81'. For geological information on the North Wales coalfield I turned to Sir Arthur Trueman, *The Coalfields of Great Britain*, London: Edward Arnold, 1954, and for details of the sinking of the Gresford shafts and of the pit's early history to *Gresford Colliery*, London: National Coal Board, 1971. I have drawn heavily for this chapter on 'Explosion of Gresford Colliery, Denbighshire: Reports', London: HMSO, 1937. Roy Palmer kindly made available to me his archive material on the disaster, and gave permission for me to quote from the reminiscences of eyewitnesses collected in 1972 and previously published in Roy Palmer's *Poverty Knock*, Cambridge; Cambridge University Press, 1974. For personal correspondence about the Gresford disaster I am obliged to Thomas Hughes, Mrs Gwyneth Jarvis (née Cartwright, to whom I am indebted for her brother Jackie Cartwright's story), H. Johnson, Mrs D. Lancelotte, D. M. Tansley and Mrs Percy Rogers. The *Wrexham Leader* kindly printed the letter that led these helpful correspondents to contact me. The *Wrexham Advertiser*, 27 September 1934, provided much valuable detail. Albert Rowlands is quoted from his article 'When Dad Was Killed in the Pit,' *Observer Magazine*, 5 December 1976, and Don Iddon from the *Daily Telegraph*. I must also acknowledge with thanks the help with this chapter given by the Geological Museum of North Wales, Bwlchgwyn, and the National Union of Mineworkers.